CW00558728

EDINBURGH AND THE FORTH

1883: 10 months

1885: 3 years

1892: 10 years

1900: 18 years

1905: 23 years

1913: 31 years

1916: 34 years

1917: 35 years

1918: 36 years

1934: 52 years

1942: 60 years

1958: 76 years

Malcolm Cant

EDINBURGH AND THE FORTH
THROUGH THE LENS OF MORNINGSIDE PHOTOGRAPHER
WILLIAM EDGAR EVANS

1882–1963

Stenlake Publishing Ltd

To the memory of
Susan McKenzie Wong
1954–2008
elder daughter of Doris and Jack Cairns

First published in 2010 by
Stenlake Publishing Ltd
54–58 Mill Square,
Catrine KA5 6RD
Telephone: 01290 551122
www.stenlake.co.uk

ISBN: 978-1-84033-495-1

British Library Cataloguing-in-Publication Data

A catalogue record for this book is available on request

Book and cover design by Mark Blackadder

CONTENTS

PREFACE

Jack Cairns

W. Edgar Evans burst into my life when I was eight years old. As a cub in the 6th Edinburgh (Charlotte Chapel) Cub Pack I attended my first Pack Holiday at Canty Bay in early July 1929. Apart from an occasional visit to Portobello beach I knew nothing about the sea-shore, so a foray into the rock-pools at low water with Pa Evans was a learning experience not easily forgotten. Similarly a walk along the coast past Tantallon Castle produced much information on birds and flowers, and a potted history of the castle. In the evening, we sat around the den fire drinking cocoa; the lighthouse on the Bass Rock sent its six flashes into the room; Pa told stories of prisoners on the Bass and of the possibility of smugglers in Canty Bay, until the cub leader chased us all off to bed. Our supper ended with a prayer of thanks for the day.

It was a legacy left to him by his father that enabled Pa finally to purchase Canty Bay from Sir Hew Hamilton Dalrymple in 1923, and until 1936 when he formed the Evans Trust he had undertaken all the expense of developing the property.

The trust deed gave the 6th Scout Group the sole right to the use of Canty Bay providing it was used for the purpose set out in the deed. Briefly, and ignoring the legal jargon, the main points are: Christian educational training to include camp-life, nature study, handwork, gymnastics, physical training of the body and the ordinary activities of a boy scout group. Military training was forbidden. 'I further declare that it is my desire that the ultimate object of the Trust should be to win the allegiance of the said boys and lads to the service of Jesus Christ and their consecration to Him as their personal Saviour and Lord.'

Pa enjoyed many hobbies and interests during his lifetime. The base for his winter activities was the top flat at No.

Jack Cairns and Pa Evans with two boys from the 6th Cub Pack in the early 1950s.

38 Morningside Park and it was here that the scouts were encouraged to join him in activities such as stamp-collecting, rearing tropical fish and of course all aspects of photography, until his death in 1963. Ethel continued to live there except for some spells of respite in a nursing home. There were a few more years when I went on taking her to Inveroran for her summer break, but she gradually became more frail and entered the nursing home permanently some months before her death in 1970.

The lawyer dealing with the estate decided that, as he knew of no relatives, I could take possession of Pa's 'History of Canty Bay', his diaries recording the development of the property and all the photographs and plates in the flat. This decision made forty years ago has, by some miracle, resulted in Malcolm Cant's excellent book.

The Scout Association has changed radically in the ninety years since Pa's first camp at Canty Bay but the trustees and leaders of today remain united in the desire to maintain this idyllic place as a living memorial to a man who could bring natural sciences alive but could also tell a good ghost story – W. Edgar Evans.

Only a few years after Pa Evans bought Canty Bay, near North Berwick, he had ambitious plans for an outlook tower. His design, dated 17 August 1926, envisaged a forty-foot structure in four, ten-foot stages on a base seven feet wide and tapering to four feet wide at the top.

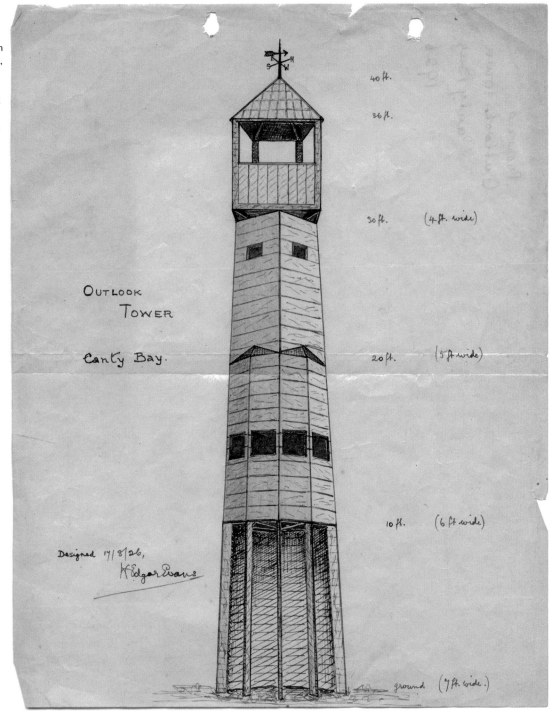

OUTLOOK
TOWER

Canty Bay.

Designed 17/8/26,
H Edgar Evans

40 ft.

36 ft.

30 ft.   (4 ft. wide)

20 ft.   (5 ft. wide)

10 ft.   (6 ft. wide)

ground   (7 ft. wide.)

INTRODUCTION AND ACKNOWLEDGEMENTS

Malcolm Cant

On 17 March 2009 I received a telephone call from one of my readers, Neil Renilson, who advised me that he had access to a large number of glass slides and negatives of Edinburgh, and wondered if I would be interested in seeing them. I met Judith and Neil at their Edinburgh flat where I viewed a selection of photographs by William Edgar Evans. From the moment that I saw the first few slides, I knew that it would be only a matter of time before this book came to fruition. I was introduced to Doris and Jack Cairns (Judith's mother and father) who had known William Edgar Evans and his sister, Ethel, for many years and had fallen heir to the photographic archive.

Over the ensuing months, I gathered in all the available glass slides, glass negatives, prints, notes and diaries and began the task of preparing them for publication. I was also fortunate to meet Margaret and George Anderson who had known the Evans family as neighbours in Morningside Park. George lent me family photographs of Evans and also from his mother's side of the family, the Deuchars of Morningside.

Edinburgh and the Forth is divided into four Parts with a short Epilogue: Part 1 deals with the Evans and Deuchar family history; Part 2 deals with Evans' adult life at Edinburgh University; his service during the First World War; his work with the Royal Botanic Garden Edinburgh; and his long association with the Boy Scouts, especially at Canty Bay near North Berwick; Part 3 is the longest part, dealing with Edinburgh; and Part 4 is a comparatively short section dealing with some of the islands of the Forth and Evans' abiding passion for Canty Bay and its environs.

I could not have produced the family section without the expert guidance of Ian Stewart, the genealogist, who also contributed to other photographs throughout the book. Alan Brotchie advised me on the transport aspects of the book jacket and Iain Macaskill of Aberlady helped with the East Lothian information. Many other people have been involved on individual subjects. In alphabetical order they are: Chris Baker; Robin Campbell; Moira and Iain Clink; Norma Gregory; Eric Hobson; Anne and Bill Hunter; Lorna Hunter; Ray and John MacKenzie; John Marshall; Charlotte Moon; Leonie Paterson; Brian Smith; Dr Anthony and Mrs Maureen Toft; and Jennifer and John Whyte.

The staff of several organisations have assisted: the Edinburgh Room of the Central Library; Edinburgh University; the Evans Trust; Faculty of Actuaries; Heriot Watt University; Historic Scotland; Mitchell Library; Northern Lighthouse Board; Royal Botanic Garden Edinburgh; Royal Commission on the Ancient and Historical Monuments of Scotland; Royal Statistical Society; and the Scottish Mountaineering Club.

As with my previous books, I received assistance from a small group of professional people without whose commitment I would be unable to get the book ready for publication: Nicola Wood did an excellent job editing the script; Mark Blackadder designed the book and the jacket to match the other books in the Pictorial Edinburgh Series; Oula Jones added a comprehensive index; and Richard Stenlake brought it all together for publication.

As always, I thank my wife, Phyllis, and the members of our extended family, including several grandchildren, for their interest and encouragement.

PART 1

WILLIAM EDGAR EVANS
AND HIS FAMILY

John Evans   m.   Charlotte Wilson   Matthew Denholm   m.   Elizabeth Walker

William Wilson Evans*   m.   Elizabeth Walker Denholm
c. 1820 – 08.5.1885   11.8.1843   c. 1818 – 11.1.1887

Elizabeth Walker E.*   Charlotte Edgar E.   John E.   Matthew Denholm E.   William E.*   Jane Romanes E.
21.2.1844 – 05.10.1925   14.8.1845 – 28.2.1943   12.3.1847 – unknown   29.7.1849 – unknown   09.5.1851 – 23.10.1922   04.4.1853 – 05.12.1900

NO
PHOTOGRAPH
AVAILABLE

Patricia Deuchar   m.   William Evans
02.9.1879

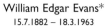

EVANS FAMILY TREE

Family tree and genealogical research by
Ian Stewart MA (Hons), Dip Ed, CSFHS

* Photographs courtesy of George Anderson

William Edgar Evans*   Charlotte Ethel Evans
15.7.1882 – 18.3.1963   26.5.1887 – 15.12.1970

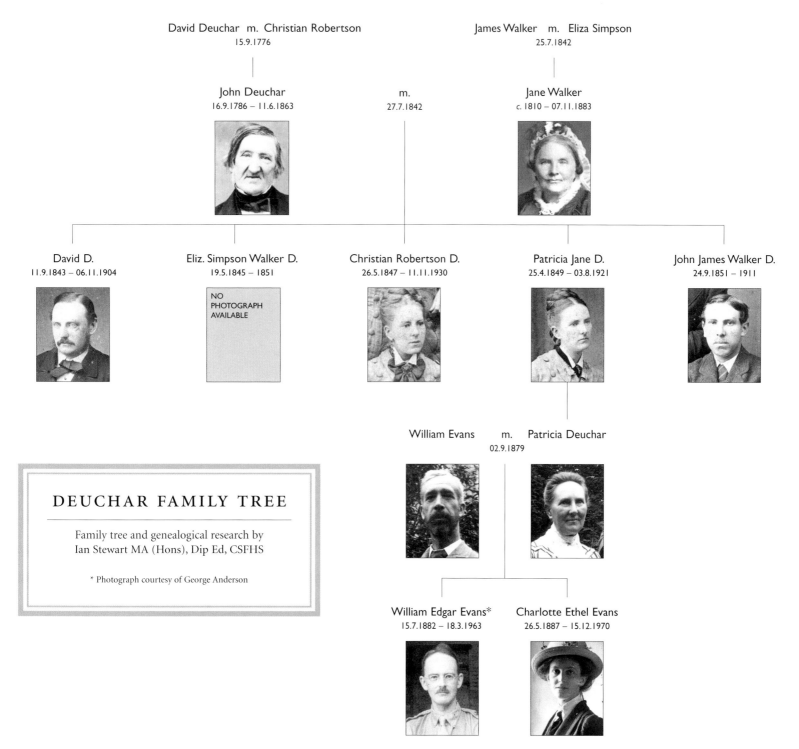

David Deuchar m. Christian Robertson
15.9.1776

James Walker   m.   Eliza Simpson
25.7.1842

John Deuchar
16.9.1786 – 11.6.1863

m.
27.7.1842

Jane Walker
c. 1810 – 07.11.1883

David D.
11.9.1843 – 06.11.1904

Eliz. Simpson Walker D.
19.5.1845 – 1851

NO
PHOTOGRAPH
AVAILABLE

Christian Robertson D.
26.5.1847 – 11.11.1930

Patricia Jane D.
25.4.1849 – 03.8.1921

John James Walker D.
24.9.1851 – 1911

William Evans   m.   Patricia Deuchar
02.9.1879

DEUCHAR FAMILY TREE

Family tree and genealogical research by
Ian Stewart MA (Hons), Dip Ed, CSFHS

* Photograph courtesy of George Anderson

William Edgar Evans*
15.7.1882 – 18.3.1963

Charlotte Ethel Evans
26.5.1887 – 15.12.1970

Eddie at 8 months, in March 1883, with his nurse. *Photograph by J. Howie, Junior, Princes Street.*

Eddie at 10 months in May 1883. *Photograph by Viewpark Photo Art Studios.*

Eddie all buttoned up, possibly for a nautical career. *Photograph by J. Moffat, Princes Street.*

Eddie's age is not recorded on the day that he was dressed as Dick Whittington. *Photograph by O. Davis, Princes Street.*

WILLIAM EDGAR EVANS:
THE PRE-SCHOOL AND SCHOOL YEARS

William Edgar Evans was born at 2.10 am on 15 July 1882 at the family home, No. 2 Merchiston Bank Terrace. He had a younger sister, Charlotte Ethel Evans, who was born at 9.15 am on 26 May 1887 at No. 18a Morningside Park. Their father, William Evans, an actuary by profession, and their mother, Patricia Jane Deuchar, had married in a Church of Scotland ceremony on 2 September 1879 at the bride's family home, No. 22 Morningside Place. The Evans family home at Morningside Park was a large semi-detached villa on the east side of the road, originally numbered 18a, but later changed to 38. It was a well-to-do family, living in a house with good accommodation and two maids to assist Mrs Evans. Like many other mothers, Mrs Evans indulged her family to the extent which the family income allowed, including fairly frequent visits to professional photographers, either on Princes Street or at Viewpark Studios which overlooked Bruntsfield Links at the west end of Warrender Park Crescent. As a child, William appears to have been called Eddie, presumably from his middle name Edgar. None of the many photographs refers to him as William or Bill.

Eddie attended a small private school in the street where he lived, run by the Misses Mackay. The Mackays, a recently widowed mother and her three unmarried daughters, came to Edinburgh in the mid-to-late 1870s. They set up the school at No. 16 Pentland Terrace before moving to No. 13 in the mid-1880s. No. 13 Pentland Terrace became No. 55 Morningside Park in 1894. It is not known at what age Eddie first attended but he was under the care of the Misses Mackay until he was 10 years of age.

W. E. Evans at home ready to enter Edinburgh University.

In 1892, when Eddie was 10, he was enrolled at the Preparatory School at Merchiston Castle. In those days, the main school and the Preparatory School were at Merchiston Tower (now part of Napier University) at the Holy Corner end of Colinton Road. Merchiston Castle School was already well established by the time young Eddie entered its portals. The school was begun in 1833 by Charles Chalmers, brother of Dr Thomas Chalmers, the famous leader of the Disruption in 1843. When Eddie joined Merchiston Castle School in 1892 the headmaster was Dr John Johnston Rogerson who had been in the post since 1863. Dr Rogerson probably holds the record for having been the headmaster longer than any other incumbent. He retired in 1898 after 35 years in the job but continued his additional duties as chairman of the board of directors until his death in 1903.

As a youngster, Eddie appears to have spent a lot of his time with a small group of friends, developing similar outdoor interests such as photography and ornithology. There is evidence that it was his mother who first encouraged him to take an interest in photography.

The maid is waiting at the doorway of the Evans
family home at No. 38 Morningside Park for the daily
delivery of milk on 2 November 1898. The dairyman
is Jas. Montgomery of Morningside who was based at
Hunters Tryst on Oxgangs Road. The cart is being
pulled by Maggie his brown pony and the milk boys
are Bob, on the left, and Davie, on the right.

The photograph, dated early 1892, is of the staff and pupils at the Misses Mackay's School in Pentland Terrace (later absorbed into Morningside Park). Eddie is on the extreme right of the second back row, and his sister, Ethel, is the dark-haired girl in the front row.

The Mackay family came to Edinburgh from the west of Scotland in the mid-to-late 1870s. The mother was Mrs Margaret Mackay (née Kennedy), a Gaelic speaker from Assynt, Sutherland, who had been recently widowed from the Rev. Hugh Mackay, a Free Church of Scotland minister at Kilmun, Argyll. Mrs Mackay was accompanied by her three unmarried daughters: Jessie Kennedy Mackay; Helen (Nellie) Falconer Mackay, a teacher; and Margaret Falconer Mackay, also a teacher. Helen lodged at No. 5 Merchiston Bank Terrace whilst the mother and the other two daughters (Jessie and Margaret, Junior) settled at No. 16 Pentland Terrace. Some time in the 1880s Helen rejoined the family at No. 16 before they all moved to No.

13 a few years later. No. 13 Pentland Terrace later became No. 55 Morningside Park. Mrs Mackay's father, the Rev. John Kennedy was a Church of Scotland minister and her brother, John Kennedy Junior, was a Free Church of Scotland minister. After the death of Mrs Margaret Mackay from cancer on 30 December 1897, the daughters, Helen and Margaret, moved to No. 16 Gillespie Crescent where three of young Eddie's aunts were living. Clearly, the Evans family and the Mackays were close friends. By 1901, Margaret Junior had stopped teaching but her sister, Helen, was still teaching in addition to being secretary to the Women's Medical College in Edinburgh. She would therefore have known and been influenced by the pioneering female doctor of the time, Sophia Jex-Blake, at Bruntsfield Lodge.

In the photograph there are three adults with similar facial characteristics, but unfortunately they have not been named. The eldest lady, with the dog on her lap, is presumably Mrs Margaret Mackay. The lady in black near the centre of the group looks older than the lady immediately behind her. On that basis, the former is likely to be the older, teaching daughter, Helen, and the lady in the back row is likely to be Margaret Junior.

The photograph was taken in the back garden of No. 13 Pentland Terrace which is now No. 55 Morningside Park. In recent years several alterations have been made to the rear of the building but there is no doubt about the location.

Above. Dr John J. Rogerson was 32 years of age when he became headmaster of Merchiston Castle School in 1863. He was a graduate of Edinburgh and London Universities and had previously been assistant master at Loretto from 1848 to 1851. *From* 'Merchiston Castle School Register, 1833–1929'.

Above right. This undated photograph shows the original Merchiston Tower in the background with the Victorian two-storey extension abutting its north wall. The 1877 Ordnance Survey map shows the outline of the Tower, the Victorian extension and the curved wall and entrance.

Right. This undated photograph is captioned 'Merchiston Castle Preparatory School'. which was started by Dr John J. Rogerson in October 1891. Initially, the school was based at Merchiston Lodge, a private house to the east of the main school. The building shown in the photograph was built in 1892 at the north end of the Merchiston Lodge garden. The upper windows of the terraced houses in Blantyre Terrace can be seen. *Malcolm Cant Collection.*

The Library, Merchiston Castle, Edinburgh

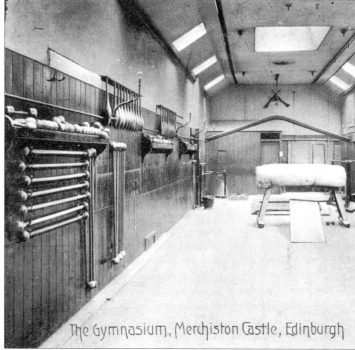

The Gymnasium, Merchiston Castle, Edinburgh

The Dining Hall, Merchiston Castle, Edinburgh

Above left. The library was built and presented to the school by Dr Rogerson at the time of his retirement in 1898. When Dr Rogerson was at the school, great improvements were made in the accommodation. He also secured a feu of 14 acres on Colinton Road from the Merchant Company which was levelled and turned into a playing field.

Above. In the early years of Merchiston Castle School there was not a great deal of emphasis on physical fitness and outdoor sports. However, this developed into a significant part of the school curriculum to include football, rugby, cricket, athletics, gymnastics and shooting. Judged by modern standards, the gymnasium in this photograph is rather sparsely equipped, but, of course, in those days most of the physical activity was confined to rather simple, repetitive drill.

Left. Compared to the library and the gymnasium, the dining room is almost sumptuous in a well lit and well ventilated hall erected in 1876. There is a top table, and there are ornamental plants and table cloths. The walls are adorned with antlers and framed pictures of senior members of staff. *All Malcolm Cant Collection.*

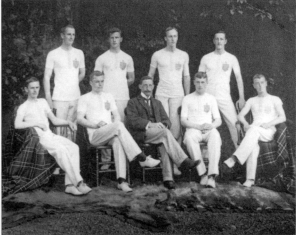

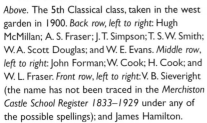

Above. The 5th Classical class, taken in the west garden in 1900. *Back row, left to right*: Hugh McMillan; A. S. Fraser; J. T. Simpson; T. S. W. Smith; W. A. Scott Douglas; and W. E. Evans. *Middle row, left to right*: John Forman; W. Cook; H. Cook; and W. L. Fraser. *Front row, left to right*: V. B. Sieveright (the name has not been traced in the *Merchiston Castle School Register 1833–1929* under any of the possible spellings); and James Hamilton.

Top right. Merchiston Castle School, Gymnastic VIII, in 1901, with W. E. Evans on the extreme left of the front row.

Centre right. The 6th Modern English class in 1901 with W. E. Evans sitting on the ground on the right.

Lower right. The 5th Classical Science class in 1899 with W. E. Evans to the left of the master.

In each of the four pictures, W. E. Evans appears to be using a cable to take the photographs remotely.

Above left. The boys are playing in a field now occupied by the houses on the south side of Hermitage Drive, in 1899. They are in what is now the back garden ground of No. 12. The building behind the boys is No. 41 Hermitage Gardens and also No. 7 Hermitage Drive, built for the Bennet family who were great benefactors to Greenbank Parish Church. The boy at the top of the pyramid is George Thorburn Addis; the boy in the centre is Tom Wise; and the boys carrying the weight are W. R. Addis (cousin of George), on the left, and Tom Fleming, on the right.

Above centre. W. E. Evans (Eddie) spent a lot of his time exploring the south side of Edinburgh and taking photographs. This is a remotely-taken photograph of himself sitting on top of the Caiy Stane (now off Oxgangs Road) in 1900.

Above right. Eddie again takes his own photograph and that of his friend, W. R. Addis, on 8 August 1898. They are at the 'Arbor', a tree-top hideout which they erected in a meadow once used by the Edinburgh Volunteers as a shooting range. The location is now part of Hermitage Drive.

Left. Eddie also sought out the Moredun and Burdiehouse lime workings as a place to explore. This self portrait, using a flashlight, is dated 1899.

CHARLOTTE ETHEL EVANS

Charlotte Ethel Evans was Eddie's younger sister, who was born at the family home in Morningside Park on 26 May 1887. In the family, she was always known as Ethel but to others, in later years, she was Miss Evans. She attended the Misses Mackay School, probably up to about age 10, but there is no record of what schools she attended thereafter. There is strong anecdotal evidence that she went either to college or university but was unable to graduate because of domestic pressures. She was an accomplished pianist which suggests that she studied music. She may also have been influenced by her teacher, Helen Mackay, to study medicine.

Much of her early life must, therefore, be deduced from the many photographs of her which have survived. Photographs, in adolescence, show that she was very sociable, at least in relation to the family environment. She is included in many photographs at home and also at various holiday locations throughout Scotland. There are a few photographs of Ethel in England but none abroad. She had wide interests, many of which suggested a leaning towards animals and the natural environment. There are pictures of her walking, cycling, sailing, camping,

sketching and attending her pets and ponies. She was also very close to her brother and took a keen interest in photography. She was not without a sense of humour – sometimes with a slight edge

Charlotte Ethel Evans, by O. Davis of No. 16 Princes Street, c. 1894, when she was seven.
Courtesy of George Anderson.

to it. In a photograph taken during a family picnic she writes on the reverse of the photograph that 'Lindsay' is not looking himself because a few moments earlier he had fallen into the burn. As a youngster she also had a theatrical bent, as she appears in a photograph in eastern costume with the caption 'Ethel as Fatima', possibly in *Ali Baba and the Forty Thieves* or *Aladdin*. Photographs of her at Morningside Park in her early 20s show her dressed very fashionably, perhaps for her twenty-first birthday or other special occasions.

There is a photograph in the Evans family archive (reproduced on page 16) which is something of an enigma. It is undated but was probably taken in 1904 or 1905, showing a large class of young girls in the garden of their nursery school. Ethel and her close friend, Ida Don, are in the photograph, looking as though they are employed as classroom assistants. It seems likely, therefore, that both Ethel and Ida were employed in education for a while at least. Tragically, Ida's young life was cut short on 13 March 1906, a few weeks before her 17th birthday when she died in Edinburgh Royal Infirmary following an operation for appendicitis.

From an early age, Ethel, like her mother and father, was a member of Morningside Parish Church on the corner of Morningside Road and Newbattle Terrace. She was on the committee of the Junior Foreign Mission and remained on the Communion Roll all her life. No doubt her faith would have been of great comfort to her at the time of the death of her parents within a comparatively short time of one another. Her mother, Patricia, died first, on 3 August 1921 and her father, William, died on 23 October 1922.

After the death of her parents, Ethel did not take up any paid occupation but managed the house and looked after her unmarried brother, Eddie. She also spent a lot of her time touring Scotland in her 1926 Morris car, taking photographs of Glen Etive, Port Appin and Castle Stalker among others. Ethel stayed at the Inveroran Hotel, Glenorchy, for two weeks every year. She would normally use her own car but latterly she hired a car and driver from Jones Motor House in Morningside Road to take her there and back.

Her literary skills also came to the fore with the publication by the Edinburgh publishers, Oliver & Boyd, in 1936, of a book of her poems under the title *The Tree and Other Poems*, which she dedicated to the memory of her mother and father. The hardback volume, running to 43 pages, contains 26 poems, many of which had previously appeared in various periodicals. Three poems, 'A Prayer for My Friend', 'Death' and 'The Princess' are very poignant, dealing with her spiritual thoughts and her earthly aspirations. Surely, 'Tears in Her Heart' refers to her friend Ida, which runs:

Tears in her heart, – how could I guess
    From her quiet face?
Was there a hint in her deep clear eyes
Of the pain that is never asleep, but cries
    In its hiding place?
She never told of those pitiless
    Tears in her heart.

Ethel, on the left, and her close friend, Ida Don, in the back garden of No. 38 Morningside Park, 1905. Ida died the following year, a few weeks before her 17th birthday.

Daily she went her steadfast way,
    Seeming so glad.
I thought I knew her – I, her friend –
Yet I never learned till the very end
    That she was sad.
I loved her; I would have kissed away
    Those tears in her heart.

Other poems, such as 'Prayers' may be a tribute to her mother and father but 'Parting' does not divulge its secret. It might have been for Ida but it could well have been for someone else:

My friend, I know the day must come
    when you will pass out of my life.
You will turn and leave me;
and I shall strain my eyes through the
    dusk for a glimpse of your face,
and listen till the last faint echo of your
    footsteps dies into the silence.

Yet I can never wholly lose you.
You that I know so well,
that sit and talk with me,
you are mine, you will stay with me
    forever.
I have shut the gates of my heart
    upon you;
you can never leave me now!

It is impossible to read Ethel's book of poems without concluding that her long life was tinged with sadness, especially in her early years, by events which changed the way she thought, but at least allowed her to express those thoughts in poetry.

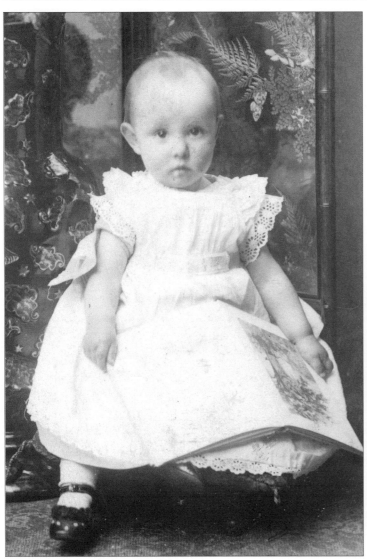

Ethel at about one year old, in 1888. *Photograph by Alexander Ayton, No. 43 North Bruntsfield Place, who also had a studio at Shipquay Place, Londonderry.*

Both Ethel and her older brother, Eddie, pose for this undated photograph. *Photograph by George Shaw, Viewpark Photo Art Studios.*

Top left. Ethel with her bicycle in the back garden of the family home at No. 38 Morningside Park, *c.* 1897.

Top centre. Ethel, standing on a small board, with what appears to be a hand puppet on her left arm, at No. 38 in 1898.

Top right. Ethel picnicking at Bavelaw, date unknown.

Lower left. Ethel sketching at Balquhidder, 1902.

Lower right. Ethel with Missie the pony at Aberlady, 1898 or 1899.

This photograph is one of the very few in the Evans archive that does not carry either the date or the location. The bay window is similar to that at the family home at No. 38 Morningside Park but that location was ruled out as there was no evidence to support the idea that Mrs Evans had ever run a nursery. After several abortive leads, it was discovered that the photograph was taken in the front garden of No. 35 Colinton Road. The two young assistants on the left of the picture are Ida Don and Ethel Evans. The photograph is likely to have been taken in 1904 or 1905 shortly before the death of Ida in 1906. Ethel and Ida were obviously very good friends although Ethel was nearly two years older. Ida was born on 7 April 1889 at No. 5 Merchiston Bank Avenue, just round the corner from where Ethel's mother and father had lived when they were first married. Ida's father was Alexander Don, a bank inspector, who moved with his wife, Joanna Jane Frederica Smith, to a much larger house at No. 26 Polwarth Terrace c. 1892. He had retired from the Royal Bank of Scotland by the time he died in May 1904, shortly before Ida's 15th birthday. Despite having lost her husband and her daughter within a short space of time, Mrs Don lived on until she was 78.

The more senior lady on the right of the photograph is likely to be Miss Brown who ran the private school from the house known as 'The Hill' at No. 35 Colinton Road. Miss Brown did not live on the premises; she lived at No. 50 Rankeillor Street.

A few years after this photograph was taken, the same school was being run by the Misses Marshall and Greig. Miss Brown ran other small schools in different parts of the city.

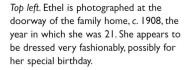

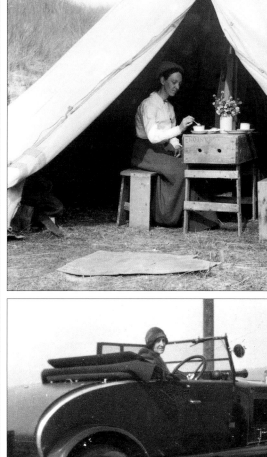

Top left. Ethel is photographed at the doorway of the family home, *c.* 1908, the year in which she was 21. She appears to be dressed very fashionably, possibly for her special birthday.

Centre. Ethel. looking quite business-like at Bradford, 1913 or 1914.

Top right. Ethel at Freshwater Haven Camp in 1914 with what her brother described as a home-made table and bench.

Lower left. Ethel adopts a thoughtful pose in this photograph taken by Alice Inglis in 1909. No definite information has been obtained on who Alice Inglis was. On the assumption that she was not part of the family of professional photographer, Alexander A. Inglis of Rock House, Calton Hill, she probably lived at either Merchiston Park or Dick Place.

Lower right. Ethel purchased a 1926 Morris car in which she toured the Highlands on several occasions. The location of this photograph is believed to be Mauricewood, Penicuik.

Top. Ethel with her parasol, hopefully to shield her from the sun rather than the wind, sitting with her brother, Eddie, on the small bench which still sits against the wall of the main building at Canty Bay, with a magnificent view of the Bass Rock. The photograph was taken on 28 June 1952.

Right. Ethel, as a spritely lady of 80, photographed on the day of the unveiling of the memorial gates at Canty Bay to her brother Eddie in 1967.

Above. The memorial gates. From *75 Years of Scouting*.

WILLIAM EVANS AND
PATRICIA JANE EVANS, NÉE DEUCHAR

Eddie's and Ethel's father was William Evans, born on 9 May 1851, and their mother was Patricia Jane Deuchar, born 25 April 1849. They were married on 2 September 1879 in a Church of Scotland ceremony at the bride's family home at No. 22 Morningside Place. Marriage in the bride's family home was the norm in those days for Presbyterians and most other Protestants. They occasionally married in the manse but very rarely in the church. Just prior to his marriage, William had moved from living with a widowed maternal aunt, who farmed at Fairmilehead Toll, to rejoin his mother, father and sisters in their new house at No. 16 Gillespie Crescent.

Patricia Deuchar was one of five children, three girls and two boys and had been living with her parents immediately before she got married. The couple's first matrimonial home was a tenement flat at No. 2 Merchiston Bank Terrace which later became No. 39 Colinton Road. This is where their first child, Eddie, was born in 1882, but they had moved to a much larger house at No. 18a (later renumbered 38) in Morningside Park, by the time Ethel was born in 1887.

The ground on which No. 38 was built belonged to David Deuchar (Patricia's brother) of Morningside who had been brought up in his parents' home in Morningside House, but had subsequently married Marion Seton Giddings and was living at Harlaw in Hope Terrace with his children and five servants, two of whom were nurses for the children. Harlaw was a very grand detached house on the south side of Hope Terrace with commanding views of Blackford Hill, Braid Hills and the Pentlands. The house was originally built for Benjamin Hall Blyth, the civil engineer. David Deuchar granted a feu charter, dated 18 May 1880, transferring five acres on the east side of Morningside Park to builders, Walter and John Kirkwood of Annandale Street Lane. W. & J. Kirkwood were builders of some note, having been the main contractors for the construction of the Royal Observatory on Blackford Hill, opened in 1896. The houses on the east side of Morningside Park were completed rather piecemeal which meant that the Evans' house was given the temporary number 18a before Pentland Terrace, on the west side, was also incorporated. The other side of the Evans' semi-detached property was owned by John Kirkwood of W. & J. Kirkwood –

which puts beyond doubt that the block was built to a high standard.

After schooling at the Edinburgh Institution, William Evans joined the staff of the Scottish Widows Fund at No. 9 St Andrew Square. He was appointed an Associate of the Faculty of Actuaries on 12 May 1873 and became a Fellow on 29 January 1877. He also published several papers including one entitled: 'On the Value of a Reversionary Annuity Payable oftener than once a Year', in 1875. The Actuarial Society of Edinburgh was also fortunate to have his support as a committee member, secretary and then vice-president at various dates between 1875 and 1887. Unfortunately, when still in his forties, William suffered severe health problems and was obliged to retire. He turned his spare time, however, to good advantage and devoted himself to 'his favourite pursuit, attaining distinction as probably the most competent field naturalist'. Despite his early retirement through ill health, William lived until he was 71. He died on 23 October 1922, slightly more than a year after his wife Patricia, who died on 3 August 1921. They are both buried in the family grave in Morningside cemetery.

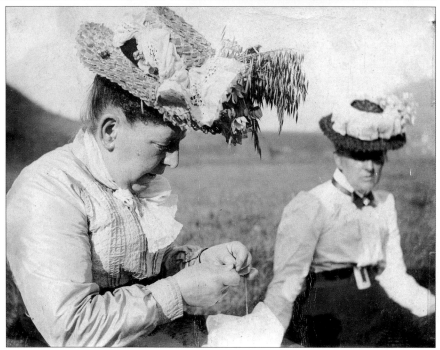

Above. Patricia Jane Deuchar, the fourth child and third daughter of John Deuchar of Morningside and Jane Walker, was born on 25 April 1849 at Morningside House. The photograph is undated but looks as if it was taken a few years before her marriage, aged 30, on 2 September 1879, to William Evans. Immediately before her marriage she was living with her parents in the family home at No. 22 Morningside Place.

Above centre. Patricia Evans is dressed for the winter in this undated photograph on the ice on the Union Canal at Kingsknowe.

Above right. Patricia is holding the family cat in the back garden of No. 38 on 1 January 1898. By then she was 48 years of age and had two children, Eddie, aged 15, and Ethel, aged 10. Her husband, William, had retired in 1892 on grounds of ill health.

Right. The photograph was taken in 1901 at Elvanfoot, Lanarkshire, during one of the family holidays. Patricia is on the right and her older sister, Christian Robertson Deuchar, is on the left. Christian was born in 1847 and lived until she was 83. She never married but took on the task of being the family historian.

Left. William Evans attending to his plants in the back garden of No. 38. Although William retired through ill health from his job as an actuary, he lived until he was 71, enthusiastically pursuing to the end his interest in botany.

Above. The Evans family archive states that this image is a photograph of a painting of William Evans entitled *The Young Naturalist* by George Paul Chalmers, who was well known for his portraits of children. The painting was probably done in the early 1860s. The entry in *The Dictionary of Scottish Painters 1600–1960* says that Chalmers' output was not large 'cut short by his brutal murder in Charlotte Square, Edinburgh', in 1878. His death certificate does not, however, confirm this: it says that he fractured his skull as a result of an accidental fall on a stair.

Above. Mrs Patricia Evans and her daughter, Ethel, are sitting on the bench while William Evans attends to the garden in the background. The photograph was taken during a family holiday at Callander in 1900.

Above right. Patricia Evans and her husband, William, photographed in their back garden on the day of their silver wedding anniversary on 2 September 1904. Eddie was 22, Ethel was 17 and most of Patricia and William's brothers and sisters were still alive which suggests that it would have been quite a big family occasion.

Right. This family group was taken in 1919 in front of William's greenhouse at Morningside Park. *Left to right*: Charlotte Ethel Evans; Aunt Lizzie (William's eldest sister Elizabeth Walker Evans); Patricia Evans; Aunt Chattie (William's older sister, Charlotte Edgar Evans); and William Evans.

THE WIDER FAMILY
AND CLOSE FRIENDS

The Evans grandfather was William Wilson Evans, son of John Evans and Charlotte Wilson, born in 1820 in Dysart, Fife. William had a great interest in plants and horticulture all his life, details of which are included in a later section of this book dealing with the Royal Botanic Garden. He married Elizabeth Walker Denholm, daughter of Matthew Denholm and Elizabeth Walker, on 11 August 1843. The Evans grandparents had six children which provided Ethel and Eddie with three aunts, Elizabeth, Charlotte and Jane, and two uncles, John and Matthew.

The Deuchar grandfather was John Deuchar, one of twelve children born to David Deuchar and his second wife, Christian Robertson. Grandfather John Deuchar married Jane Walker on 27 July 1842 and between them they produced five children, one of whom, Elizabeth, died as a child. From the Deuchar side, therefore, Ethel and Eddie had two uncles, David and John, and one adult aunt, Christian. Grandfather John came from the well-known family who held royal appointments in the crafts of seal engraving and lapidary work. It was John's father David and his younger brother, Alexander, who established the business. John did not follow them into seal engraving but studied science and wrote several scientific papers. In 1826 he was made a burgess of the City of Edinburgh, a distinction conferred on him because his father had

John Deuchar of Morningside House, maternal grandfather of Eddie and Ethel Evans. The photograph was taken shortly before his death on 11 June 1863. *Courtesy of George Anderson.*

held the same office. By the 1830s, he was enjoying the life of a landed proprietor in Morningside House, a detached property on the west side of Morningside Road between what is now Morningside Park and Springvalley Gardens. Before the Deuchars, Morningside House was occupied by a senator of the College of Justice, Lord Gardenstone, portrayed in Kay's *Original Portraits* as 'distinguished as a man of some talent and much eccentricity' riding into town on horseback with a young boy in Highland dress running behind. The boy was employed to look after the horse during the time that the court was in session, and then to run all the way back to Morningside at the end of the day. One of his even more eccentric habits was to warm his bed in the winter by getting his pet pig to lie in it before he retired for the night. Presumably he was working on the premise that even if the law was not an ass, at least it was close to a pig!

Colourful as the story undoubtedly is, it might well be apocryphal. Ethel Evans noted the tale in her copy of *Historic Morningside* by William Mair and added the rather droll comment that in her Scots dictionary the word 'pig' refers to a stone hot-water bottle!

The photographs are of Eddie and Ethel's maternal grandparents. The grandmother, Jane Walker, was born in 1810 to James Walker, a printer, and his wife Eliza Simpson. Jane Walker was living at No. 18 Buccleuch Place when she married John Deuchar of Morningside House on 27 July 1842. There was a considerable disparity in their ages as Jane was a mere 32 whereas John was 55. Interestingly, at the time of the 1841 census (taken only a year before) John stated that he was 45 whereas he was actually 54. Whether he transposed the numbers accidentally or as a prelude to his impending courtship will never be known. Either way, in just over nine years, he and his wife produced three girls and two boys.

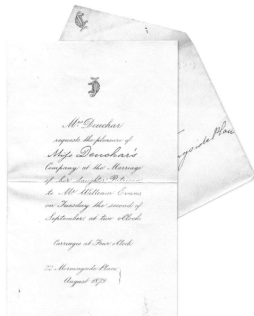

Left. This Deuchar family photograph is undated but is probably *c.* 1880, a few years before the death, in 1883, of Mrs Jane Deuchar who is in the centre of the picture, surrounded by her family. In order of year of birth they are: David, born 11 September 1843 (*back right*); Christian, born 26 May 1847 (*front left*); Patricia, mother of Eddie and Ethel, born 25 April 1849 (*back left*); and John, born 24 September 1851 (*front right*). There was another child of the family, Elizabeth, born 19 May 1845 who died aged six.

Above. Christian Robertson Deuchar was always known as the family historian. She certainly lived up to that title by retaining this item and passing it on to her descendants. It is a wedding invitation that has survived still in its original envelope. It is from Mrs Jane Deuchar to her elder daughter, Christian, inviting her to the wedding of the younger daughter of the family, Patricia, to 'Mr William Evans on Tuesday the second of September at two o'Clock'. The phrase, 'Carriages at Four o'Clock' was a polite way of telling the guests, in advance, when they were expected to go home.

Above left. Mrs Elizabeth Walker Denholm, born *c.*1818, died 11 January 1887. She married William Wilson Evans on 11 August 1843. She was Eddie and Ethel's paternal grandmother. Eddie would have remembered her but Ethel was born after she had died.

Above centre. William Wilson Evans, born *c.* 1820, died 8 May 1885, married Elizabeth Denholm. He is seen here with his son, John Evans, the uncle of Eddie and Ethel. *Courtesy of George Anderson.*

Above right. John Evans, born 12 March 1847, is the gentleman on the left. He was the older brother of Eddie and Ethel's father, and, therefore, their senior uncle on the Evans side of the family. The identity of the other man is not known.

Right. Jean or Jane Romanes Evans was born on 4 April 1853 and died on 5 December 1900 at Bank House, Braeside in Liberton Parish. She was the youngest aunt of Eddie and Ethel on the Evans side.

Far right. The three Evans aunts at an unknown location. *From left to right:* Jean (Jane); Charlotte (Chattie); and Elizabeth (Lizzie).

The Addis family is photographed very informally with their two dogs, *c.* 1903, at an unidentified location. At the time, they were living at No. 34 Hermitage Gardens but the photograph does not appear to have been taken there. It shows: *back row, left to right*, Mr David Foulis Addis, born 26 April 1849; Dorothy Scott Addis, born February 1891; and George Thorburn Addis, born November 1885. *Front row, left to right*: Ronald Forrester Addis, born September 1896; Eric Elrington Addis, born May 1899, but not looking very boyish in the photograph; Emily Frances Malcolm (Mrs Addis) born October 1860; Annie Addis, born May 1884; and David Malcolm Addis, born 10 February 1882. David Foulis Addis was the son of the Rev. Thomas Addis the founding minister of Morningside Free Church, established shortly after the Disruption in 1843, when many ministers and members of the congregations left the established church over the question of patronage in the appointment of ministers.

David, and his wife Emily Frances Malcolm, who came from a Scottish family living in Liverpool, married on 7 January 1879 in Shahjahampur in India, where David was an official in the Indian Civil Service. As a graduate of both Edinburgh and Glasgow Universities, and having been successful in the Civil Service examinations in 1870, he was obviously destined for a successful career. When he arrived in India in 1872 he was appointed as an assistant magistrate but 25 years later when he retired he was a District and Sessions Judge. During his time in India, his three middle children were born. He

returned to Edinburgh in 1896.

The Evans family and the Addis family were known to one another but the extent of the friendship in uncertain. Eddie and David Malcolm Addis were about the same age, had similar interests and probably met for the first time at Merchiston Castle School. The school register records David Malcolm Addis joining the Preparatory School in 1891 at a time when

the remainder of his family was still in India. In the 1901 census, David is described as a 19 year-old architect's pupil. Details of his subsequent career have not been discovered but he enlisted as Private Addis in the City of London Regiment, regimental number 7078, and was commissioned as a 2nd Lieutenant in the Royal Fusiliers on 19 July 1916. Tragically, in the fierce fighting on the Western Front he was

posted 'Missing' on 9 June 1917. As his body was never identified he does not have a personal

grave but he is commemorated on the Menin Gate Memorial at Ypres.

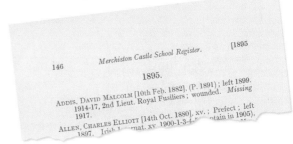

Merchiston Castle School Register.   [1895

146   1895.

ADDIS, DAVID MALCOLM [10th Feb. 1882], (P. 1891) ; left 1899.
    1914-17, 2nd Lieut. Royal Fusiliers ; wounded. *Missing*
    1917.
ALLEN, CHARLES ELLIOTT [14th Oct. 1880], xv. ; Prefect ; left
    1897. Irish I_____ rnat. xv 1900-1-3-4- _____ ptain in 1905).

PART 2

UNIVERSITY, WAR YEARS, WORK AND SCOUTS

EDINBURGH UNIVERSITY
AND HERIOT WATT COLLEGE

William Edgar Evans entered Edinburgh University in 1901, at the age of 19, directly from Merchiston Castle School. According to the *Edinburgh University Calendar 1906–07*, Evans received his degree of Bachelor of Science in Pure Science on 28 July 1905 with Special Distinction in Botany. Nine names are recorded (including Evans) with a larger group for 12 April 1906. Students were reminded that they could apply for various post-graduate scholarships. Evans applied to the secretary of the Carnegie Trust, Merchants Hall, Hanover Street, Edinburgh and was awarded a Carnegie Fellowship of £150. He spent the following two years on research at the Royal Botanic Garden at Inverleith. The results of his research were published in 1909 in a paper entitled 'On the Further Development during Germination of Monoco-tyledonous Embryos; with Special Reference to their Plumular Meristem'.

In 1908 when he had completed his time with the Royal Botanic Garden he was appointed to the teaching staff of Heriot Watt College, which, at that time, was in Chambers Street in the building now occupied by the Crown Office. The college principal was Dr A. P. Laurie and

Evans was appointed as assistant to Dr Emil Westergaard who was in charge of Technical Mycology. The various courses were designed to appeal to a wide range of students, many of whom later went to Edinburgh University to sit a B.Sc. degree. The potential occupations included: margarine manufacturers; brewers; distillers; and maltsters. One of the

Edinburgh University students, July 1903, with Evans on the extreme left of the front row.

categories of students wishing to enrol in special or advanced courses was described as: 'Students engaged in industries subjected to the disturbing influences of micro-organisms, such as gelatine, starch, sugar, preserve-making, and who desire to obtain a general knowledge of the nature of such disturbances, so as to become more able to cope with them'.

Evans continued in his role as assistant to Dr Westergaard until 1916 when he was conscripted under the Military Service Act of 1916. He was enlisted on 2 March 1916. On 17 January 1917, after Evans had begun his training, Dr Westergaard wrote a glowing reference in which he confirmed that Evans had experience in lecturing to students on systemic mycology and bacteriology and had also given laboratory instruction in those subjects. He also mentioned that Evans had been assisting in making the bacteriological preparation which the Medical Research Committee was about to try against dysentery in a military hospital. He concluded the reference by saying that Evans was 'a thoroughly competent and experienced bacteriologist with a wide and thorough scientific training'.

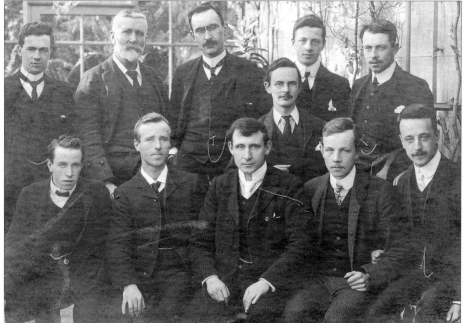

Above left. The Tower Room laboratory in 1905 with Dr Clerk Rankine.

Above top right. Petrie dishes, 1911, which Evans used along with many other slides for his lectures while at Heriot Watt College.

Above right. Sterilising apparatus for moist chambers, 1911, also used by Evans for his lectures while at Heriot Watt College.

Left. Nine students and two members of staff pose for the photograph which was probably taken by Evans himself who is the only person in the middle row. Unlike most of Evans' photographs, this one is not dated and does not have a caption. It is most likely to be a graduation photograph as there were nine students who received their degrees on the same day.

THE FIRST WORLD WAR

William Edgar Evans was 34 years of age when he was enlisted on 2 March 1916 under the Military Service Act of 1916, but he was not mobilised until 16 October. He was classified Medical Category B1 which meant that although he could serve overseas, he would be restricted to garrison duties only, rather than front line service. He was ordered to join the 2/6th Battalion of the Royal Highlanders (Black Watch) then based at Norwich where he was made Private 5388 and posted to C Company.

By late January 1917, Evans completed an application to be commissioned as an officer, backed, no doubt, by Dr Westergaard's glowing reference from Heriot Watt College in Edinburgh. His application was specifically to join the Sanitary Section of the Royal Army Medical Corps. His background in botany, mycology and bacteriology made him especially suited to work involving the sanitation of water and ensuring clean operating practices. He was discharged from the ranks on 4 March 1917 and was commissioned as a lieutenant on 5 March.

Evans sailed from Devonport on 30 August 1917 and arrived at Basra in what was then Mesopotamia (now Iraq) on 18 October. He travelled up the River Tigris to Baghdad and took command of 46 Sanitary Section of the Royal Army Medical Corps. He appears to have made a good impression as he was promoted to the rank of captain on 5 March 1918. Later that year, 46 Sanitary Section moved from Mesopotamia up into Persia (now Iran).

The year 1919 was eventful for Captain Evans. Late in 1918 he had been admitted to No. 32 British General Hospital in Amara suffering from diarrhoea. He was again admitted to hospital, this time at Kermanshah, on 29 January 1919 suffering

Lt. Evans sent this photograph home to Morningside Park to let his family see what it was like in Amara, on 4 December 1917. Evans' office was on the left of the picture and that of the 17th Sanitary Section was on the right, as seen from the verandah of the courtyard.
Courtesy of George Anderson.

from dysentery. By 2 February he was placed on a 'dangerously ill' list but fortunately began to recover over the ensuing weeks. He left Basra on 18 April 1919, having been in Beit n'Ama Hospital there, and sailed via Alexandria and Le Havre, arriving at Southampton on 22 June, en route for the 2nd Scottish General Hospital in Edinburgh.

Evans had applied on 4 January 1919 for demobilisation in order to resume his civilian occupation, but presumably his illness had delayed the decision. However, in August 1919 he submitted a further request for demobilisation which was confirmed on 8 September 1919, enabling him to accept a post with the Royal Botanic Garden in Edinburgh.

During Evans' service in Mesopotamia and Persia, he took a great many photographs, several of which he converted into glass slides when he returned to Edinburgh. As the sole officer in his unit it was also his responsibility to maintain the official diaries, which have also survived. Written in pencil, their legibility is now diminishing, but there is no mistaking the regular, neat handwriting, signed off with his customary monogram.

Above far left. Private William Edgar Evans in the uniform of the Black Watch on 25 December 1916. He was enlisted on 2 March 1916.

Above second left. In January 1917, Evans applied for a commission in the Sanitary Section of the Royal Army Medical Corps. He became Lieutenant Evans on 5 March 1917.

Above third left. Evans saw service with the Royal Army Medical Corps in Mesopotamia (Iraq) and Persia (Iran) between 1917 and 1919. He is seen here on 23 May 1918, as Captain Evans, on the roof of the billet occupied by the Assistant Director of Medical Services.

Above. Evans is in the centre of this group of men from the Medical Corps but, unfortunately, no date or location has been traced.

Left. Lt. Evans on his Douglas motor cycle on the north bank of the River Tigris, Amara, on 16 February 1918.

The photographs on this page and the following pages have
been selected from several albums of negatives taken when
Evans was in Mesopotamia. The captions have been taken
verbatim from Evans' own notes.

Above. Amara: Turkish refugees on vessel from Bagdad (sic).
Tigris Front. 5.11.17.

Amara: Arab children, including Hamid.
Artillery Road. 21.11.17.

Above. Arab women and children breaking brick for pathmaking. Amara. 18.1.18.

Right. Arab labour overseer and boy worker, brick breaking gang. Amara. 18.1.18.

Far right. Amara: Street scene off Municipal St. showing typical houses and children. 14.1.18.

Left. Myself, on ridge among marshes 12 miles below Amara. 29.5.18.

Top right. Woman carrying firewood. Amara. 12.2.18.

Above. Capt. W. E. Evans with an Arab farmer and his workers. Amara. 1918.

THE ROYAL BOTANIC GARDEN

Three generations of the Evans family were closely involved in the work of the Royal Botanic Garden at Inverleith.

William Wilson Evans was born in 1820 in Dysart, Fife. When he moved to Edinburgh as a young man he lived at various addresses near the east end of Princes Street before taking up a job at the Experimental Gardens at Inverleith. By 1851 he was curator of the Royal Caledonian Horticultural Society's Garden before it was incorporated into the Royal Botanic Garden, where he was in charge of eight men and two boys. A few years later he progressed further by moving to the main farmhouse at Tynefield, near Dunbar. Here he farmed 265 acres with the assistance of eight men, eight women and three boys. By the early 1870s he had made another move to Bank House, Penicuik where he was land steward and factor to the Clerks of Penicuik. Evans and his wife, Elizabeth Walker Denholm, had six children, one of whom, William, born in 1851, also developed a strong interest in botany, even although it was not his main occupation.

William Evans, born on 9 May 1851 at the curator's house at Inverleith, was the fifth child of William Wilson Evans and Elizabeth Walker Denholm. As a young man he entered the insurance industry and qualified as a Fellow of the Faculty of Actuaries in Scotland while employed by the Scottish Widows Fund. Unfortunately, while still in his forties, he was required to retire on grounds of ill health. However, he turned the setback to good advantage by enthusiastically taking up his love of the natural sciences and became Scotland's foremost field naturalist of his day. William Evans and his wife Patricia Deuchar had two children, William Edgar and Charlotte Ethel.

Against such a strong background in horticulture it is hardly surprising that William Edgar Evans (and to a lesser extent his sister Ethel) took an avid

W. E. Evans, to the right of the man wearing a light-coloured hat, is showing a party of botanists round a private garden near Dollar, in 1942.

interest in botany. As a child, no doubt his father would have taken him on numerous occasions to the Royal Botanic Garden, and during his university years he would have returned in a more professional capacity. He did his Carnegie Fellowship there between 1906 and 1908, researching on the development of monocotyledonous embryos, but it was not until he was demobilised from the Royal Army Medical Corps in September 1919 that he began a long and satisfying career with the Garden. John Frederick Jeffrey had held the position of curator of the herbarium until 1917 when he needed to retire because of failing eyesight. Professor Isaac Bayley Balfour, Keeper of the Garden, solved the staffing problem by writing to Evans on 31 July 1919 offering him the job and saying: 'The sooner you come to us the better we shall be pleased'. Evans remained in the post until his own retirement in 1944. During his twenty-five years at Inverleith, he named George Forrest's vast collection of plants from the Himalayas and China, and also his own collections found in Persia and Mesopotamia. In 1924, William Edgar Evans was elected a Fellow of the Royal Society Edinburgh for his services to botany.

W. E. Evans was a member of No. 2 Fire Squad at the Royal Botanic Garden on 26 June 1942. The team members were: *from left to right*; W. Halley; James Shanks; W. E. Evans; and James Chisholm. William Halley was married to Mary Allan Ritchie and died in 1949 at the age of sixty-six. James Shanks was married to Mary McIntosh and died in 1970 at the age of ninety-two; and James Chisholm was the widower of Euphemia Trotter and died in 1950 at the age of seventy-nine.

The building at the back is the corridor which leads to the lecture theatre. Just visible behind the men is one of two fossilised Pitys trees in the possession of the Royal Botanic Garden. They were uncovered with another three from Craigleith Quarry sometime between 1835 and 1865. They had been there for 320 million years.

Above. In 1942 when No. 2 Fire Squad was not 'pitting oot fires', they employed themselves gainfully in their allotment nearby. *From left to right:* W. E. Evans; James Chisholm; W. Halley; and James Shanks.

Right. Arboretum Cottage, or the Curator's House, was the birthplace, in 1851, of William Evans, father of William Edgar Evans. At the time, W. E. Evans' grandfather, William Wilson Evans, was the curator. The building still exists as the lodge house to the East Gate, and is about to be renovated as a new reception area. *Courtesy of George Anderson.*

THE BOY SCOUT MOVEMENT

The Boy Scout Movement was begun in England by Lord Baden-Powell in 1908, by which time W. E. Evans was 26 years of age. Evans was, therefore, never a cub or a scout but in later life he took a very active interest in the movement. He was attached to more than one troop but it is probably true to say that his greatest involvement was with the 6th Edinburgh at Charlotte Baptist Chapel in Rose Street. In scouting circles, W. E. Evans was always known as 'Pa' Evans, a homely description which exactly fitted his long relationship with the youth movement. His life-long association with Charlotte Chapel is recorded in great detail in *75 Years of Scouting: The Story of the 6th Edinburgh (Charlotte Chapel) Group* written by Angus H. MacLeod, and published in 1995 by John Donald Publishers Ltd., of Edinburgh.

In his book, Mr MacLeod records that on 24 September 1919, at a meeting of the Sunday School Committee, a suggestion was put forward to establish a Boy Scout troop at Charlotte Chapel. The chairman of the committee wrote to Evans a few weeks later asking if he would be interested in leading the proposed troop. Unfortunately, Evans declined as he was already the scoutmaster at the 5th Edinburgh Central Hall troop, a post which he had taken up after a spell with the 19th Edinburgh troop, attached to the Edinburgh Industrial Brigade Home for Working Lads in Ponton Street, and also with the 8th North Edinburgh (University Settlement) troop. Happily for the Charlotte Chapel, Mr Evans reconsidered his position the following year, 1920, when he was appointed as scoutmaster at the Chapel. His suitability for the task was never in doubt, summarised by Mr MacLeod in the following words: 'He was a baptised believer, a member of the Chapel, a man experienced in camping and Scouting, a naturalist and a photographer,

At the 8th University Settlement troop's camp at Newport in 1910 Mr Price takes advantage of all available facilities for his morning ablutions. Most of the furniture appears to be made of Coutties' biscuit boxes from Dundee.

a former army officer who had served his country in the war and, perhaps not least, a bachelor of 38 without the pressures of family life and so time to give to the work'.

Although it is true that Evans had the time to devote to the troop, his own personal life was not without incident. His mother, to whom he had been very close, died on 3 August 1921, when Pa Evans was absent from home at one of the Canty Bay scout camps. The following year, his father, who had been ill for many years, died on 23 October. In April 1922 Evans resigned temporarily as scoutmaster and then permanently in October 1923 when responsibility for running the troop passed to James Bethune. Fortunately, the Chapel appointed Pa Evans to the position of Honorary Scoutmaster, in which capacity he was able to continue his close involvement with the troop. He continued to devote his energy and natural ability to teach to establishing Canty Bay, near North Berwick, as a base for many future scout camps, both for the Chapel scouts and other troops. The first cottage at Canty Bay had been rented in 1921 but in the ensuing years, Evans spent a lot of time and money gradually acquiring ownership of most of the Bay.

Right. Scouts of the 19th troop, Edinburgh Industrial Brigade Home, advertising 'A Special Matinee' at the Royal Lyceum Theatre on behalf of the Scott Antarctic Fund on Wednesday 26 February 1913. The Home was in Ponton Street and the boys appear to be standing outside the building in Thornybauk first used as a power station for Edinburgh's cable car system and later as a depot for the electric trams.

Below. Carrying the daily supply of water was a fairly arduous task at the E.I.B.H. camp at Gullane in 1912.

Below right. Leaders and boys of the 6th Edinburgh Charlotte Chapel troop stand in the traditional square formation around the flagpole on Easter Sunday morning at Canty Bay in 1938.

Left. The farmer looks on as two of his strong working horses cope with several members of the 5th Central Hall troop at Oxton, Berwickshire, in 1915.

Below left. Pa Evans, not in scout uniform, is on the right of the picture with the 6th Charlotte Chapel troop near Heriot on 3 July 1941.

Below right. An Edinburgh policeman, with helmet and white coat, waves the lorry through as it emerges from South Charlotte Street onto Princes Street. The boys of the Charlotte Chapel troop have a long journey ahead of them to Moniaive in 1949.

PART 3

EDINBURGH

THROUGH THE LENS OF MORNINGSIDE
PHOTOGRAPHER WILLIAM EDGAR EVANS

Opposite.
As Evans concentrates on his subject at Duddingston, his
friend, Alexander Milne, captures the moment, in 1901.

William Edgar Evans took a very large number of photographs of Edinburgh, most of which he converted to three-inch glass slides or transparencies. He meticulously annotated each slide with the date, location and frequently the names of the people who were in the photograph. He also maintained an index notebook in which he often included further details, e.g. of the type of film used or the weather conditions at the time that the photograph was taken.

A very few photographs in Part 3 were not actually taken by Evans, but mostly he was present at the time, and it was probably his camera that was used. It is, therefore, a safe assumption that he had a direct input into almost all the photographs, even though he may not actually have released the shutter. His earliest pictures are dated 1898 when he was 15 or 16 years of age. Most of these were taken fairly close to his own home, e.g. at Fairmilehead, Swanston, Buckstane and Hermitage of Braid, whereas others were taken further afield, at places such as Craigmillar Castle and Bavelaw, near Balerno. It may well be that his earliest photographs were taken from the upper windows of the family home at No. 38 Morningside Park. On page 79 there is a picture taken by Evans on 28 January 1898 (when he was 15) showing the first signs of building operations for the construction of Springvalley Terrace. During his photographic excursions, he was frequently accompanied by his mother, father and sister, all of whom appeared in the pictures from time to time. His father is in photographs at Fairmilehead and Caiystane, and his mother appears at Craigmillar Castle and Greenbank. Mrs Evans also took a few photographs herself, notably of Greenbank Cottage in 1908 and Buckstane Farm in 1906 where her husband's ancestors had farmed. She was sufficiently pleased with the Buckstane Farm photograph that she later reproduced it as a Christmas card. Evans' father, the naturalist, also accompanied his son to Loganlee in the Pentlands while he was studying rare mosses in that area. A few photographs were taken by Evans' close friend, David Malcolm Addis, in 1899. The pictures of Corrennie Gardens and the curling pond off Braid Road are all the more poignant when it is remembered that young Addis was killed in action during the First World War. A very few photographs by non-family members have found their way into the Evans archive, usually because Evans was present or closely involved in some other way. Alexander Milne took an excellent picture in 1901 at Duddingston Loch of

As a young photographer and naturalist, Evans was acutely aware that his surroundings in Morningside were at risk from the threat of impending development. When his mother and father moved to their new house in Morningside Park in 1884, much of Morningside Road was still lined with single-storey cottages and several smiddies. The photograph shows the view from No. 38 Morningside Park, looking north.

Evans photographing a swan and David Deuchar (Evans' uncle) took a very early photograph of his own home, Morningside House. One of the most interesting pictures in Part 3 is the photograph of Evans at the gates of Comiston House in 1901. Previously it had been thought that the photograph might have been taken remotely by Evans himself, but the archive states quite clearly that the photographer was W. Millar.

Topographically, Evans took more photographs of the south side of Edinburgh than of any other part of the city. Unfortunately, he did not cover Leith, nor any of the areas to the north of Princes Street. Part 3 commences with Duddingston and Craigmillar and moves south and west in an arc to include Liberton, Fairmilehead, Swanston, Buckstone and Oxgangs, before going further west to Loganlea, Bavelaw and Colinton. There are also pictures of Blackford Hill, the Braid Hills, Hermitage, Greenbank, Comiston and Morningside. Evans also took a most interesting series of photographs in 1938 when one of the scout troops with which he was involved went on a boating trip from Leamington to Ratho, and back. Another of Evans' specific projects was to photograph various parts of the city during the royal visit of King Edward VII in 1903. Part 3 concludes with a photograph of the Old Town from Salisbury Crags in 1899.

Chronologically, Evans' work on

In the spring of 1900, the trees are still bare and some of the undergrowth has been removed to reveal the area being made ready for the construction of tenement buildings in Springvalley Terrace. The houses nearest the camera probably had an address in what was then Rosewood Place, now part of Cuddy Lane. Comparing the photograph with the *Ordnance Survey* map of 1852 confirms that the building to the left of centre, with the additional pitched roof to the left, is Springvalley House. A stone plaque, depicting Springvalley House, was inserted on the front of the north-most tenement in Springvalley Terrace when it was built on the site of the house in 1907. Also in the photograph, the houses of Morningside Place can be seen in the background. Other views from the back windows of No. 38 appear on page 79.

Edinburgh is a bit of an enigma. He started in 1898 and took photographs during most years up until 1910. No Edinburgh material has been traced for the 1920s but in 1938 he undertook the Union Canal project. In 1953, when he was past his 70th birthday, he decided to revisit the locations of his earlier photographs. This has provided an excellent selection of 'before and after' views, especially near his home in Morningside. The areas covered include Fairmilehead, Oxgangs, Buckstane, Braids and Hermitage. Thanks to one of the wonders of modern technology, 'Google', his story of the 'Waterproof Jim Tree' in the Braidburn Valley is now available for all the world to read.

William Edgar Evans was greatly attracted to places of antiquity for his photographic excursions but he also included quite a lot of groups of people. The captions for these have been greatly enhanced by research done by Ian Stewart, especially on page 66 where the story behind the two delightful photographs of children has now been unravelled.

Right. Swans and coots appear to be adapting reasonably well as Duddingston Loch freezes over during the winter of 1900. The loch has always been a natural haven for a wide range of fish, wildfowl and other birds. It was not until 1925, however, that the area was officially designated Duddingston Bird Sanctuary after the loch and its environs were gifted to the nation by William Haggerston Askew of Ladykirk. Since 1925, a great many species of birds have been recorded, including the bittern, peregrine falcon, golden oriole, herons, pochard and greylag geese. In 1971, ground to the south of the loch was acquired to create Bawsinch Nature Reserve which provides a further buffer zone against encroaching development.

Right. A few months later, in early 1901, the ice has all gone but the trees are still bare. The building in the centre of the picture, near the water's edge, is the octagonal-shaped curling house designed in 1823 by William H. Playfair for the Duddingston Curling Society, who made him an honorary member to show their appreciation. The upper floor of the building was used as a studio by Duddingston's most renowned minister, the Rev. John Thomson, who was an excellent landscape artist as well as a pastor.

To the right of the picture, behind the trees, is the tower of Duddingston Kirk, parts of which date from the twelfth century. It is likely that the oldest parts of the building are the nave and chancel. The manse is off the picture to the right.

These three photographs at Duddingston Loch appear to have been taken by Evans on the same day during the winter of 1900. The photograph, *left*, with Arthur's Seat in the background shows that the ice on the loch is sufficiently bearing to support a large crowd of people. In the middle ground, several sightseers have lined the edge of the low road between Duddingston Village and the Park Road entrance at St Leonard's.

The lower photographs show the popularity of making slides – spills and all. Duddingston Loch was the birth place of the Duddingston Curling Society in 1795. The Society still exists but it is many years since they played regularly at Duddingston. Its motto is: *Sic Scoti: alii non aeque felices* – This is the way the Scots play: the rest of the world isn't half so lucky.

Above left. Evans describes this climbing scene on Salisbury Crags as 'a very good hitch', in 1902. The climbers are, *from left to right*: Gall Inglis; Harold Raeburn; and W. E. Evans — waiting to see just how good the hitch is before he begins to climb. No one is wearing protective headgear. Gall Inglis was a member of the Inglis family, who ran the firm, Gall & Inglis, cartographers, famous for *Shorter Spins Round Edinburgh* and other route maps.

Above right. Of the three climbers photographed on Salisbury Crags, the most experienced, by far, was Harold Raeburn, who was born on 21 July 1865 at No. 12 Grange Loan. His father, William, was the main proprietor of W. & J. Raeburn, brewers, of Merchant Street. Harold and his brother, John, joined the firm, by which time it had moved to Duddingston, where it was later taken over by Youngers. Harold Raeburn was a great yachtsman and

mountaineer, having been part of the Everest expedition in 1921 during which he took ill. He never really recovered his health after that and died in Craighouse Hospital on 21 December 1926, the causes of his death being recorded as 'Exhaustion from melancholia' and 'Endocrine insufficiency', the duration of both illnesses being recorded very precisely as '4 years 10 months and 13 days'.

Left. Craigmillar Castle, photographed from the west in 1898 (when Evans was 16 years of age) probably with Mrs Patricia Evans on the right of the picture. Parts of the castle date from the late fifteenth century, the barony of Craigmillar having been acquired by the Preston family in 1374. The Gilmour family lived there from 1660 until the end of the eighteenth century when they moved to the Inch.

Below left. In either 1899 or 1900, Evans photographed the fireworks factory at Craigmillar quarry. The buildings seen in the picture appear very modest compared to the hype generated by the firm's extensive advertising in 1894. In those days, a fireworks factory was laid out in a series of small, isolated buildings to reduce the likely extent of damage and injury in the event of an explosion.

Below. Hammond's advertisement gives a very grand impression of the business. *Malcolm Cant Collection.*

Manufactory—CASTLE WORKS,
CRAIGMILLAR, DALKEITH ROAD, EDINBURGH.
The most Complete Fireworks Factory in Scotland.
Licensed as per Act of Parliament.
SIGNAL ROCKETS and BLUE LIGHTS, for Steamers and Sailing Vessels, as required by the Board of Trade. Several Hundred Pounds' worth always in Stock.

T. HAMMOND, MANUFACTURER.

FIREWORKS FOR PRIVATE AND PUBLIC DISPLAYS,
in all their Beauty and Dazzling Brilliancy.

By the recommendation of a number of my Patrons, I am now making up Cases of Selected Coloured Fireworks, ranging in Price from 10/6 to £20, with instructions to fire them.

Please send for List of Contents of Cases.

For GARDEN PARTIES and CHILDREN'S FETES.

I supply Balloons elaborate in shape and Colour; also curious and comical Birds, Beasts, and Fishes; also Ally Sloper, Fat Policeman, Mr Punch, and other shapes.
A BALLOON, WITH FIREWORKS ATTACHED, for 5s.
ILLUMINATION LAMPS FOR SALE OR HIRE.
CHINESE LANTERNS and ALL REQUISITES for ILLUMINATION

The Cheapest House in the Kingdom for Good Fireworks.
Several Tons of Fireworks always in Stock.

Post Address—**16 EAST MAYFIELD, Dalkeith Road.**

This group of scouts, led by a slightly apprehensive-looking leader, is collecting for the Scott Antarctic Disaster Fund in 1913. Robert Falcon Scott, known as Scott of the Antarctic, commanded two Antarctic expeditions, one from 1901 to 1904, and the second from 1910. He and his entire party died in 1912 on the return journey, having been beaten to the South Pole by his Norwegian rival, Roald Amundsen.

The scouts in the photograph are from the 61st troop attached to the Edinburgh Industrial Brigade Home. Initially, there was some doubt as to whether the photograph was taken at Upper Liberton (near Liberton House) or Nether Liberton. The boys are, in fact, at Nether Liberton, on Gilmerton Road, near its junction with what is now Liberton Road. The houses on the right have long since been demolished but were very near to Good's Corner which still survives. The square building, to the right of the telegraph pole, is Nether Liberton doocot, dating from the fifteenth or sixteenth century. It was probably built by the proprietors of Inch House, now on the east side of the main road. The doocot is believed to be the largest in Edinburgh, measuring approximately 37 feet by 20 feet. It is built on the lean-to, or lectern, principle, with two main chambers.

Left. Liberton Brae has always been a challenge for cyclists and heavily-laden carts. The driver has alighted and is leading the horse, but, for some unknown reason, he is not using the specially laid track on the left which has smooth gutters for the cart wheels and rough inlay to give the horses's hooves a better grip. The photograph is dated 1902.

Below left. The undated photograph is captioned, 'Milk cart at Bank House, Liberton'. The cart is very similar to Montgomery's milk carts seen on pages 6 and 59 of this book. The lady in the picture is Charlotte Evans, aunt of William and Ethel, whose picture appears along with two of her sisters on page 26.

Below. The undated photograph is of Peter Burnell in the manse grounds at Liberton. The only Peter Burnell found in the United Kingdom census for 1901 was a 57-year-old retired brewer's drayman of No. 13 Buckingham Chambers in the City of Westminster. His connection with the manse at Liberton has not been discovered.

Top. The photograph is captioned, 'The Luggie, Morton Road', and is dated 5 January 1898 when Evans was only 15 years of age. His father, William Evans, probably assisted him as he is in the picture on the left. The Luggie was the small thatched cottage on the corner of what is now Frogston Road West and Winton Drive.

Above. When Evans returned in March 1953 to take a photograph from the same spot he was 70 years of age. Much had changed, but the two photographs can be aligned with one another by comparing the position of the trees, especially the unusually shaped tree to the left of the two men walking on the pavement.

Right. The Luggie was clearly one of the Evans family's favourite locations for photography. This picture, taken in 1908 by Mrs Patricia Evans, features Miss Charlotte Ethel Evans, the daughter. Although she is well dressed for the winter, her footwear hardly seems adequate for the conditions. In 1908 there was no bus service from Morningside to Frogston Road West and the family did not have a car. Horse trams were extended to the Braid Hills Hotel terminus in 1897.

Above. The Caiy Stane looks particularly isolated in this photograph, dated 27 January 1898, looking south-west towards the Pentland Hills. The hedgerow running across the picture marks the position of Oxgangs Road, long before any houses were built there. The information board now erected at the Caiy Stane, by the National Trust for Scotland, states that the stone may have been erected as early as the Neolithic period, possibly before 3000 B.C., to denote a ritual or burial place.

Far left. On the same day, 27 January 1898, the photograph includes William Evans. The picture appears to have been taken in a slightly more westerly direction, looking towards Hunters Tryst and the plantation of trees known as the Cockit Hat at the east end of Redford Road.

Left. The Caiy Stane photographed in its 'modern' setting on 27 March 1953 on the east side of Caiystane View.

Top left. Hillend, as the descriptive name of the farm, is recorded from 1526 according to *The Place Names of Edinburgh* by Stewart Harris. Evans photographed it on 17 April 1899 from the road leading to Flotterstone and Biggar. In recent years some of the outbuildings had fallen into disrepair but they have now been extensively renovated.

Top right. In 1898 this cluster of thatched cottages was the centre of Swanston village. The two-storey building, with the lower part of the gable in shadow, is the village school, attended by the local children and some from as far afield as Bowbridge, Lothianburn, Comiston House, Fordel and Dreghorn. When the school closed in 1931, it was bought by Mrs Boyd, the last person to teach at the school.

Above. In March 1953 Evans returned to take the same view again. After 55 years the two photographs are remarkably similar.

Above. This wintry scene of the T wood and the Pentland Hills was taken in April 1908 from Oxgangs Road. The T wood was laid out by Henry Trotter of Mortonhall in 1766. Although seen as T-shaped from Edinburgh, it is actually in the form of a Maltese cross, which detracts a little from the assertion that the wood was planted by Trotter (T for Trotter) to assert dominion over water rights. An Act of Parliament of 1758 permitted Edinburgh Corporation to use spring water from Swanston to increase the public water supply from Comiston Springs. Trotter objected, saying that he needed the water for his own use, and that, in any case, the Corporation would not need more water if its existing pipes did not leak so badly. The case was heard by the Sheriff Court which ruled in favour of the Corporation. On appeal to the Court of Session and the House of Lords, the Sheriff Court decision remained unaltered.

Above left. The Shepherd's Cottage was photographed in 1901, and, *left*, Evans returned in March 1953 to photograph it from a slightly different angle. Unfortunately, by the mid-1950s many of the thatched cottages had fallen into disrepair. In 1956 an ambitious scheme, originally estimated at £17,000, was put forward by the City Architect for conversion of nine old cottages into seven renovated dwellings. By 1960 the eventual cost of renovations was nearer to £26,000 but an excellent result was achieved which has been maintained to the present day.

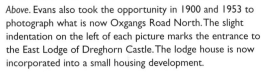

Above. Evans also took the opportunity in 1900 and 1953 to photograph what is now Oxgangs Road North. The slight indentation on the left of each picture marks the entrance to the East Lodge of Dreghorn Castle. The lodge house is now incorporated into a small housing development.

Above right. Hunters Tryst at the west end of Oxgangs Road dates from about 1800. It is shown by that name on Knox's map of 1812, displacing a previous name, Sourhole. When the present Hunters Tryst building was called Sourhole, the name Hunters Tryst was applied to a completely different hostelry a short distance to the south of Fairmilehead. It is not known whether the name, Hunter, describes the clientele or was the name of the proprietor. The photograph is dated 27 January 1900.

Right. Towards the end of his life, Evans returned to the scene of many of his earlier photographs. This one is dated 3 March 1953, by which time the corner had gained a direction sign, A70 to Lanark and A71 to Midcalder.

Top left and right. Both photographs show James Montgomery, the dairyman, at Hunters Tryst in 1900, one with his horse bridled, and the other with full harness to draw the milk cart. The 1901 census, taken less than a year after the photograph, states that Hunters Tryst had eight rooms, with windows, and was occupied by James

Montgomery and his wife, Ellen. They had the assistance of a teenage dairymaid and a teenage vanman. James and his wife Ellen, née Winward, married on 10 December 1895 at Tattonhall, County Chester. Their daughter, Ellen Winward Montgomery, was born on 18 April 1899 at No. 9 Millar Crescent.

Above. Montgomery's two milk carts are drawn up ready for the photograph at the bend in the road (now Oxgangs Road) south-east of Hunters Tryst. The child on the extra horse is presumably young Ellen. The quiet country road has been changed out of all recognition, now lined with houses on both sides of a wide thoroughfare.

The two photographs illustrate how many of the small paths and rights of way disappeared as the district of Oxgangs was developed. The left-hand picture was taken in 1902 looking eastwards from the path that ran between Dreghorn and what is now Oxgangs Road North. The Comiston Springs Cistern House can just be seen in the middle distance, with the Braid Hills in the background.

In the right-hand picture, taken in March 1953, the scene has lost some of its charm. The building on the right is an electricity sub-station (extant) and part of a pre-fab can be seen to the left of the central telegraph pole.

The stone wall marks the boundary of the paddock surrounding Oxgangs farmhouse, later converted to Oxgangs Police Station.

The top picture shows Oxgangs farmhouse in 1899 with the Pentland Hills in the background. When Evans revisited the scene in 1953 some of the trees on the left had disappeared but those on the right had grown substantially. Otherwise, the layout of the farmhouse and outbuildings remained largely unchanged. Oxgangs farmhouse was a substantial building of nine rooms but on census night in 1901 the only occupant recorded was the 46-year-old housekeeper, Mary Mossman. The farmhouse is now occupied as Oxgangs Police Station.

During Evans various photographic excursions to the south of his home in Morningside, he was greatly attracted to the remaining farmhouses, steadings and cottages. He would have known that Buckstane farm was at one time tenanted to his paternal great-grandfather, Matthew Denholm. At the time of the 1881 census, Buckstane was still being farmed by John Evans (paternal uncle of William Edgar Evans) on behalf of Jane Romanes, the 76-year-old aunt of John Evans.

Above left and right. Evans first photographed the building on 5 January 1898. The stonework on the front of the building suggests that at some time previously it had been raised from one storey to two. By the time that Evans returned on 28 March 1953 the steadings on the right had been converted to living accommodation.

Right. Evans mother, Mrs Patricia Evans, was also attracted to the building as a photographic subject. She took this picture in 1906 and used the image on several occasions as a Christmas card.

Above left. This historically important photograph, showing the words Comiston House on the pillars, has appeared in previous publications, notably *Historic South Edinburgh* by the late Charles J. Smith and *South Edinburgh* by the present author. Now that the original slide has been found in the Evans archive, it transpires that the photograph was not, in fact, taken by W. E. Evans. In many similar locations he took the photograph remotely so that he would appear in it. The archive states quite clearly that it is W. E. Evans in the photograph but that it was taken by W. Millar in 1901. The caption, dated 1901, is in Evans' own neat handwriting but rather oddly says, 'W. E. Evans, age 17, in the foreground'. In 1901 Evans was 19.

Above. The corresponding photograph in March 1953 shows the site of Comiston House pillars which by that time had been moved from Comiston Road to the north entrance to Braidburn Valley Park. The pillars which marked the approach to Comiston House, at the east end of Camus Avenue, have been moved on two occasions. Edinburgh City archives hold drawings, dated 9 February 1923, to widen Comiston Road and reposition the gates to the north-west. It was also necessary to move the wash house from the east side of the lodge to the south. The second move was about a decade later when the gates and pillars were dismantled and moved to Braidburn Valley Park. In the photograph, the small street sign 'Camus Avenue' can be seen on the right.

Left. To complete the story, Evans took this photograph in March 1953 at the entrance to the park.

This evocative scene of the ruined cottage is described by W. E. Evans as 'Head of Loganlee, below Nether Habbie's Howe 1906'. At the time, Evans was 24 years of age and was accompanied by his father, William Evans, the naturalist, who was researching rare species of moss found at Loganlee. It may be William Evans who is leading the horse. His work was published in the *Botanical Journal of Scotland* and other publications.

Above left. Evans does not identify the boys in this interesting group. His caption is very brief: 'Boys with Fire, Torduff, Pentlands, 1910'.

Above. George Davidson, the gamekeeper, Easter Bavelaw, in 1901.

Far left. Keeper George Davidson, Easter Bavelaw, and his family, 1898. The lady is his wife, Ann, and one of the boys is presumably his son George, who would have been 15 years of age when the photograph was taken.

Left. Waterfall at Nether Habbies Howe, at the head of Loganlee, 1906.

These delightful photographs were taken at Bonaly Farm, Colinton, in 1901. Somewhat disappointingly, Evans gave the photographs very brief captions: on the left, 'Schoolgirls, Bonaly Farm, 1901' and, on the right, 'Cumming & Cowe, Bonaly Farm, 1901'.

Thanks to present day research by Ian Stewart, we possibly know more about the photographs now than Evans did more than a century ago. There is a strong facial resemblance between the girl on the left of the photograph and the boy on the left of the other photograph. A similar resemblance can be seen between the girl on the right and the boy on the right. In each case they are, in fact, brother and sister.

The 1901 national census was taken only a few months before this photograph. There were several workers' cottages at Bonaly, two of which were occupied by the Cumming and Cowe families. Andrew Cumming, a 37-year-old ploughman, lived with his wife, Rosina, and their children: Andrew, aged 16; Hugh, aged 11; Catherine, aged 9; and Charles, aged 5. A nearby cottage was occupied by William Cowe, a 48-year-old shepherd, with his wife, Agnes, and their children: William, aged 9; and Mary Ann, aged 7.

The photographs, therefore, show: *from left to right*; Catherine Cumming, aged 9; Mary Ann Cowe, aged 7; Hugh Cumming, aged 11; and William Cowe, aged 9, but looking quite small for his age.

Above. This scene of desolation is all that remains after a fire at Kate's Mill, Colinton Dell. The photograph is dated 1900 but the fire occurred in 1890. The paper mill was built in 1787 by John Balfour & Sons, booksellers in Edinburgh, the mill being named after John Balfour's wife, Catherine Cant of Thurston. The mill took its power from a long lade taken off the Water of Leith from a broad weir, upstream towards Colinton. Although nothing now remains of the mill, Kate's Mill Cottage, seen to the left of the tall chimney, still exists as an attractive dwelling.

Left. Dreghorn Castle was probably built by Sir William Murray, Master of Works to King Charles II in the mid-seventeenth century. It lay in extensive wooded policies between what is now Redford Loan and the City Bypass. After falling into disrepair it was finally demolished with the use of explosives on 1 May 1955.

The three images on this page, all dated 1913, have been reproduced from slides on which Evans had experimented with colour techniques. There is also a little bit of doubt about whether the location is Redhall or Redford. In his index book, Evans records all three photographs at Redhall but his captions, written on the actual slides, are as follows:

Right. Charlotte Chapel, Sunday School Picnic, Redhall, Water of Leith, 1913.
Below. Charlotte Chapel, Sunday School Picnic, Redford, Water of Leith, 1913.
Below right. Charlotte Chapel, Sunday School Picnic, Redford, Water of Leith, 1913.

Above. The Boy Scout Movement was begun in England by Lord Baden-Powell in 1908 with emphasis on, *inter alia*, outdoor activities. These ideals were taken up enthusiastically by the leaders and boys of the 8th North Edinburgh (University Settlement) troop. They are seen here 'scirmishing' (sic) in 1910 on Blackford Hill. Little did they know that reality was not far off. During the First World War, 1914-18, many young men, possibly some of these, lost their lives on the Western Front and other theatres of war.

The Royal Observatory, in the background, was designed in 1892 by W. W. Robertson of H. M. Office of Works. Its east and west towers are clearly visible with the library wing between them. The house of the Astronomer Royal is on the extreme left of the picture.

Left. This picture, probably taken on the same day in 1910, shows the boys of the 8th troop marching on Blackford Hill. The topography looks like the high path above Blackford Pond, leading towards Corbie's Crag.

Above. During January 1903 many skaters were drawn to the pond on the Braid Hills. It lay to the south of the old road between Braid Road and Liberton, part of which can be seen in the top right-hand corner of the photograph. No doubt much to the relief of the golfers, the skating pond was drained in the mid-1920s when the old road was abandoned and rebuilt to its present position further north.

Right. In this photograph, dated 23 March 1956, it is not difficult to see the similarity in the topography but the area previously covered by the skating pond is now part of the golf course. The old road has also disappeared leaving only a narrow access pathway.

Above left. Evans took this photograph in 1898 and gave it the caption, 'Fall, Braid Hermitage, haunt of Dippers'. He took many photographs of birds' nests and the natural habitat of wildlife in general. At the Hermitage of Braid, the fall, or weir, was created artificially to raise the water level to a lade which in turn powered a mill wheel. Charles J. Smith in *Historic South Edinburgh* alludes to the mill which was operating as early as 1695 as a corn and paper mill.

Above. Evans returned on 23 March 1956 to record the same location which was largely unchanged.

Left. However, a short time later Evans took this photograph of the stretch of the Braid Burn immediately downstream from Hermitage House. Evans records that the scene of desolation was caused when the weir and fall were washed away by a storm during January 1957.

The mansion of Hermitage of Braid was built in 1785 for Charles Gordon of Cluny. The design, probably by Robert Burn, in a romantically defensive style, has mock machicolations, battlements and even pointed, dummy bartizans on the corners. It was Charles Gordon who was responsible for laying out the grounds with lawns and various species of trees. The old walled garden, the lectern-style doocot and the ice-house are extant, but the corn mill to the west of the house has long been demolished. After the Gordons ceased to live at the Hermitage, their trustees let the property to several tenants, including Sir John Skelton, the advocate. The house and grounds were purchased by John McDougal from the trustees for £11,000 and in 1938 were gifted to the city as a public park. In more recent years, the house has been used as a scout hostel and is now a visitors' centre and base for the Countryside Ranger Service.

This view is one of the most interesting in the Evans' collection of small prints. The print was never converted to a glass slide, probably because it was not taken by Evans himself. It is likely that he was present when the photograph was taken in 1899 by his friend, David Malcolm Addis, from the upper windows of the Addis family home at No. 34 Hermitage Gardens. The shadow of the roof and chimneys of No. 34 can be seen in the foreground of the picture. Details of the Addis family are given on page 27: David Malcolm Addis was killed on the Western Front during the First World War.

The house in the centre of the photograph is No. 18 Corrennie Gardens. It is more or less completed but does not yet appear to be occupied as the lower left-hand window is still boarded up and the garden is full of building materials.

The feuing plan for the area, by Rowand Anderson, is dated 16 November 1897 and the house architect was Sydney Mitchell. Several well-known Edinburgh tradesmen were involved in the construction: James Millar & Sons, builders, of Millar Place; Patrick Knox & Son, plumbers and gasfitters, No. 1 Montpelier Park (with a simple telephone number, 62); D. F. Wishart & Co., iron merchants, No. 18 Picardy Place; and William Anderson & Son, slaters, No. 91 Haymarket Terrace. The house was named, 'Monar', and was first owned by Charles Moxon of Moxon & Carfrae, gilders and picture restorers, No. 77 George Street. The two-storey, L-plan, Arts and Crafts villa, B listed by Historic Scotland on 30 March 1993, is described as of exceptional avant-garde design.

The photograph also shows, on the extreme left, the large detached house, Rubislaw, at the top of Braid Avenue which was demolished many years ago for the construction of the present-day flats.

The right-hand foreground of the picture shows the roofs of No. 41 Hermitage Gardens and No. 7 Hermitage Drive, which also appear on page 11. Rather remarkably, when the present owners of No. 41 Hermitage Gardens bought the house in recent years, the hand roller, seen propped against the boundary wall, was still in position.

Top left. Braid Burn curling pond was photographed by David Malcolm Addis in the spring of 1899. Again, Evans was probably with him when the photograph was taken. No records of the curling club have been traced but it seems likely that it existed between 1890 and around 1914. Margaret Warrender, author of *Walks near Edinburgh* in 1895 refers to the club's existence but does not give any further details.

Top right. Evans returned on 23 March 1956, without his friend David who had been killed in the First World War, to photograph the same scene. By that time the curling pond had long since been drained and Mortonhall Tennis Club had laid out their courts. Curling Pond Cottage was extant and was used for a while by the club as a club house. The tennis courts were laid out in 1914.

Above left. Evans photographed the adjacent Braid Burn Dairy in January 1898 when he was 15 years of age. The dairy lay north of the curling pond almost opposite the entrance to the Hermitage of Braid in Braid Road.

Above right. Again, Evans returned on 23 March 1956 to photograph the site of the old dairy, by which time it had been long demolished. There is, however, no mistaking the location.

Top left. The thatched cottage at Greenbank has been photographed on many occasions, in various seasons, and frequently with the occupants standing at the front door. This study, by Mrs Patricia Evans in 1908, is slightly different as the acute angle enables us to see the alignment of Fly Walk better. Although the cottage looks quite idyllic, it was really very basic with no electricity, no gas, no running water and only earthen floors. It was usually occupied by the workers at Greenbank Farm. The cottage stood on ground which later became the back garden ground of Nos. 17 & 19 Greenbank Crescent, built by David Adamson of Morningside Road in the first decade of the twentieth century.

Lower far left. Evans' caption for this photograph is 'Salix alba, Braid Burn and Comiston Springs, 1908'. Early photographs of Braid Burn valley show several similar willow trees but at the present day many of the originals have been lost to old age and storm damage. The cistern house at Comiston Springs can be seen to the right of the tree.

Left. When Evans returned to the location in March 1953 the willow tree had disappeared, and the houses built on Comiston Farm were creeping down the hill. Rather unusually for Evans he added a short anecdote to the slide: 'We used to play here about 1893 [when he was aged 11] and the tree, the Waterproof Jim Tree, was named after our waterproof satchel'. Apparently the satchel was temporarily lost one day near the tree but was found again on a later visit. This 1953 photograph is also cross-referenced 'see photos of theatre in 1901 and 1903'. Unfortunately, the theatre photographs have not been found in the archive.

Above. The steadings of Comiston Farm lay a few hundred yards to the south of the cistern house. The steadings have long since been demolished but the large, square farmhouse still stands on the corner of Swan Spring Avenue and Pentland Drive. The photograph was taken on 3 February 1900.

Above right. This undated photograph shows Mrs Patricia Evans on the small footbridge over the Braid Burn near the south entrance to the present day public park. The bridge gave access to a path, Cockmalane, which still runs due south towards Swanston, and also a separate right of way to Oxgangs and Colinton Mains which has now disappeared.

Right. Mrs Patricia Evans looks slightly overdressed for working in the fields at Comiston Farm in 1904. Fortunately, the harvest has been cut and the stooks of corn have been stacked to dry in the sun.

Comiston Farm resisted urban development for much longer than Greenbank Farm which succumbed in the early 1930s. Comiston Farm was still being run as a going concern until the mid-1950s when the Harwell family, who ran the tea-room at Colinton, feued out the remaining acres for house building.

Evans described this photograph as, 'Morningside Road Station with trace horses under the lamp'. One version of the photograph is dated 1899 and the other 1900. The better opinion is 1899. To the left of the central lamp standard are: the North British Railway Morningside Road Station; J. D. Lawson, coal merchant; and J. Macdonald & Co., sculptors, who also had another yard at Canal Bridge, Leamington Road.

On the left of the photograph there is a horse-drawn tram, the lower part of which is obscured by a horse and cart. The tram carries an advertisement, 'Crawford's Biscuits: Always the Best' and the board immediately below it says, 'Newhaven, Post Office, Morningside Drive'. In fact, from 18 December 1897, the horse tram terminus had already been extended from Morningside Drive to a new terminus on Pentland Terrace below the Braid Hills Hotel. Cable cars replaced the horse-drawn trams on this route from 26 October 1899. The tram in the photograph is to a design built at Shrubhill between 1886 and around 1894: the first tram of this design won a gold medal for the Edinburgh Street Tramways Company at the International Exhibition of Industry, Science and Art held on the Meadows in 1886. Towards the right of the picture there are two trace horses which were used to pull the tram up the steep incline of Comiston Road.

The three photographs on this page are a major contribution to the visual history of old Morningside. The clarity of the originals is not as good as Evans' own slides but they are still worthy of inclusion.

Above. The reverse of the small photograph of Morningside House says it was taken by David Deuchar in the 1860s (see pages 23-25 for photographs of the Deuchar family). It is carefully annotated to identify each of the buildings. *From left to right:* Morningside House; joiner's shop with the trestle outside; Free Church School, with the open window shutters; and the smiddy, behind the small cart.

Above right. This undated photograph by Evans is captioned 'The Smiddy, Old Morningside, which stood on the site of Morningside Public Library'. The smiddy, owned for many years by the Denholm family, can be traced back to at least 1832: it was demolished prior to the construction of the library in 1904.

Right. The third photograph, undated, is of Paradise Cottages, described on the reverse as 'off Morningside Road, at the end of Jordan Lane'. Charles J. Smith in *Historic South Edinburgh* says that the cottages lay between Jordan Lane and Canaan Lane at the back of the Volunteer Arms. On *Johnston's Plan of Edinburgh*, dated 1851, the cottages are not named but could be the block, lying north to south near the site of the police station.

These two contrasting views were taken within a few months of one another from the upper windows of the Evans family home in Morningside Park.

Left. Evans' own caption is : 'View E. from 38 Morningside Park, Edin. Cow park and byres of J. Reid's dairy: first signs of building operations visible: 28.1.98'. In fact, there appears to be only a small amount of disruption on the right of the picture. The foreground shows the roof of the kitchen or scullery of No. 38, and the background shows tenements in Morningside Road.

Left. A great deal has changed in this later photograph. Evans' caption is: 'View E. from 38 Morningside Park, Edinburgh. Remains of Reid's cow park and byres: tenements well advanced. Summer 1899'. The newly-built tenement on the right is the beginning of the east side of Springvalley Terrace.

In May 1938, the crew members of the *Alice* are all ready for a boat trip at the Leamington end of the Union Canal. The boys are, *left to right*: Alex Howieson, Bertie Brown, Walter Howieson and Peter Brown. The Leamington lift bridge, seen on the right, has been renovated in recent years and now opens again to allow increased waterway traffic along to the redesigned Lochrin basin. The Union Canal was designed by Hugh Baird as a contour canal, without locks, five feet deep, twenty feet wide at the bottom, and thirty-five feet wide at the surface of the water. The cost was estimated at £235,167 but by the time it was opened in May 1823, the cost had risen to £461,760. It never aspired to carrying as much freight or as many passengers as had been hoped, mainly because it was eclipsed by the Edinburgh and Glasgow Railway within twenty years of its opening.

The photograph also gives an excellent impression of the extensive buildings of the North British Rubber Co. Ltd. Their products were legendary, but in case anyone did not know, the tall chimney stack carried a vertical advertisement [RUBB]ER TYRES. The company was established in 1856 by Henry Lee Norris and was famous for its range of products which included boots, shoes, motor car tyres, belts, combs, golf balls, hot water bottles and rubber flooring. The company also produced ground sheets and anti-gas curtains during both World Wars.

Unloading coal from a barge on the Union Canal, near Slateford, looks like warm work despite the canal being partially frozen over in January 1902. The exact location of the photograph is not stated by Evans, but there are only two points west of Slateford where the railway line crossed over the canal. The photograph is, in fact, at the bridge nearer to Slateford where there was a loop line off the Caledonian track coming from the Caledonian Station at the foot of Lothian Road. The loop crossed over the Union Canal and then over Lanark Road before entering Colinton Dell, en route for stations at Colinton, Juniper Green, Currie and Balerno. Beyond Balerno, the loop rejoined the main line to Carstairs Junction at Ravelrig Junction. The Balerno line carried passengers up until 1943 and freight until 4 December 1967 when the closure of the last two mills made the line completely uneconomical.

At the present day the location and the bridge can still be identified. The photograph was taken, looking eastwards towards Slateford, a few hundred yards west of the bridge which once carried the loop line over the canal but is now a pedestrian walkway. On the extreme left of the picture, a short section of railing marks the spot where there is still a tunnel (partially flooded by water) which allowed the quarrymen access to workings on both sides of the canal. On the right of the picture, the two chimney stacks belong to the semi-detached dwellings, Redhall Bank Cottages (at one time known as Millbank Cottages) designed and built in 1857 by James Gowans, architect and quarry owner, for his workers.

Above. The crew of the *Alice* has now reached the aqueduct which carries the canal over Slateford: Walter Howieson is surveying the scene from the tow path; Alex Howieson has both hands on the ropes; Peter Brown is considering his next move in the centre of the boat; and Bertie Brown is enjoying the journey.

Right. Stoneyport lay west of the aqueduct and had landing stages on both banks of the canal. It was on the south side of the canal, a few hundred yards nearer to Slateford from the location seen on the previous page. The building has long since been demolished but stood on Lanark Road almost opposite the entrance to Redhall Walled Garden. A large quantity of stone from Hailes Quarry was conveyed by barge into Edinburgh for house building. When Hailes Quarry was eventually abandoned in the twentieth century, it was 120 feet deep and was already beginning to fill with water.

Far right. Evans took many interesting photographs but he also had an eye for the seemingly mundane. The railings at the east end of the aqueduct have been worn away by mooring ropes over many years. As the aqueduct is much narrower than the remainder of the canal, boats would probably be moored temporarily at one end waiting for an oncoming boat to pass.

The crew has arrived at Gogar and the boys are having a well-earned tea, May 1938. The original crew of four has been increased to six. The two additional members, who may have been on another boat for the journey, are R. Armstrong, with his legs outstretched on the left, and James Howieson, biting a sandwich, nearest to the camera.

Hailes Quarry had produced an immense amount of building stone by the time this photograph was taken in 1901. Most of the activity is in the right-hand corner where men are cutting at the face and the derricks are in position to move the heavy stone. Hailes Quarry was producing fairly large quantities of stone as early as 1750 which eventually supported a substantial industry before starting to go into decline in the nineteenth century. Three distinct colours of stone were produced: the lower levels produced a dark grey stone; the upper levels produced a red stone; and in various beds a blue tint was located. Grey stone was used for Dalry School in 1876, Lochend School in 1886 and Sciennes School in 1891; blue stone was used for Plewlands Villa, Morningside, in 1878; and red stone for Red House, Cluny Gardens, in 1880.

Right. Workings at the upper end of Hailes Quarry near the Union Canal in 1901.

The photographs on this page and the following two pages were taken by W. E. Evans when Edinburgh was decorated for the visit by King George VII after his coronation in 1902. He came to the throne on 22 January 1901 on the death of his mother, Queen Victoria, who had reigned since 1837.

Top left. Evans added a comment to this photograph: 'Owing to the King's sudden illness there was a delay of several months in the functions'. The photograph shows a cable-car bound for Gorgie coming under the arch bearing the words, 'Long Live Our Noble King', at the west end of Princes Street.

Left. Also in 1922, the heavily laden cart is making its way eastwards on Princes Street at the junction with Hanover Street. The shop on the left is Thornton & Co. at No. 78 Princes Street. The business of patentees, waterproofers and india-rubber manufacturers was established in 1848 and had branches in London, Leeds, Bradford and Belfast.

Above. The premises of Henry, Darling & Co., silk mercers, at No. 124 Princes Street was elaborately decorated as a ship with the words, 'Ye Good Ship King Edward VII' across the projecting window.
All courtesy of George Anderson.

Above. A stylishly dressed pedestrian on Princes Street with the decorated Royal Scottish Academy behind.

Above right. Outside the North British Hotel (now the Balmoral) the very impressive archway has individual panels for: New Guinea; Newfoundland; India; Australia; Ceylon; Cape Colony; New Zealand and Tasmania.

Right. The bowler-hatted gentleman on the right appears to be using his handkerchief rather than his mobile phone. The vehicle on the extreme left caught the attention of Evans who describes it as 'the primitive motor vehicle that had begun to give a public service from Waverley to Haymarket'. *All courtesy of George Anderson.*

Above. When Edward VII and Queen Alexandra arrived at Waverley Station on 11 May 1903 their route to Dalkeith Palace was by North Bridge, East Preston Street, Dalkeith Road, Cameron Toll and Bridgend. This section of roadway, south of Minto Street, would only have been used by the royal entourage on their way to subsequent engagements in Edinburgh.

Above left. In Bristo Place, the corner premises, occupied by the long-established china merchants, John Donald, are elaborately decorated as befitted their status 'By Appointment to His Majesty'.

Left. The Bore Stone, situated on the boundary wall of the original Morningside Parish Church in Morningside Road, was also bedecked with a flag. At the time, Evans was living nearby at Morningside Park and would be very familiar with the location.

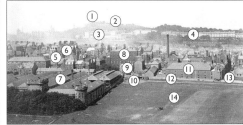

1. Nelson Column
2. National Monument
3. Royal High School
4. Regent Terrace
5. Stack for the Holyrood Flint Glass Works
6. Milton House School
7. Park Ale Stores
8. Queensberry House
9. Lodge to Queensberry House Hospital
10. Pavilion
11. Abbey Brewery
12. South Back of the Canongate (now Holyrood Road)
13. Horse Wynd
14. Royal High School Cricket Ground

This image is taken from a small print with the caption, 'Edinburgh from Arthur's Seat, 1899'. The reverse of the print has the name, Dr Inglis Clark, but it is not clear if he was the photographer or the owner of the print. The information for the accompanying numbered grid has been extracted from the Ordnance Survey map of 1896, surveyed only a few years before the photograph was taken.

PART 4

THE FORTH

THROUGH THE LENS OF MORNINGSIDE
PHOTOGRAPHER WILLIAM EDGAR EVANS

Opposite.
A full boatload of sightseers from *P. S. Redgauntlet*
arrives on the Isle of May in 1911. Further details
of *Redgauntlet* appear on page 97.

Part 4 includes some of the photographs which Evans took on the islands of the Forth, at Gullane, Aberlady and Gosford, and, particularly, at Canty Bay. He did not set out to complete a comprehensive study of every part of the Forth. In total there are fewer photographs in the archive for this part of the book than there are for Part 3 which dealt with Edinburgh. In addition to that, most of the illustrations for the Forth are associated with Boy Scout camps which Evans organised for many years. Nonetheless, it is an interesting collection of photographs taken between 1898 (when he was 16 years of age) and 1956 when he was well past his 70th birthday. Not only did Evans photograph the Boy Scout campers at work and play, but he established friendships in many of the neighbouring localities.

There are three islands included, all within easy access of Canty Bay, namely the Bass Rock, Craigleith Island and Lamb Island, and, quite a bit further into the Firth of Forth, the Isle of May. For young boys, and for the adults too, the Bass Rock must have been a very exciting place to visit. It has, of course, a fascinating history which, no doubt, Pa Evans would narrate to the boys during the voyage. The Bass is a very majestic volcanic plug rising 350 feet above sea level, about three miles to

Evans refers to this slide quite briefly as 'Gipsies' Encampment, Boglehill, 1898'. Boglehill was at the area known as the Bents near the shore at Longniddry. It seems more likely that the travellers were tinkers rather than gipsies: Evans may well have looked upon the two descriptions as interchangeable, whereas, historically, their origins are quite separate.

the east of North Berwick. Landing steps have been formed on the east and west sides which Pa Evans would have used when the weather was sufficiently calm for the trip to be made. One of the great attractions was the variety of sea birds that colonised the rock, including guillemots, gannets, fulmers, puffins, kittiwakes and many more. In addition to its ornithological attractions, the Bass had many nooks and crannies for the boys to explore, including its lighthouse on the east side, established in 1903 and designed by David A. Stevenson, which cost just over £8,000 to erect. Of much more ancient origin were, of course, the ruins of St Baldred's Chapel, believed to date from between the end of the fifteenth century and the early sixteenth century.

One of the other islands included in Evans' photographic study is the round islet of Craigleith, which appears to have been visited by the boys on numerous occasions, possibly because of its comparative accessibility, about a mile off shore from North Berwick. There are photographs of the boys arriving at the small landing stage, and also on the summit, which is much less impressive than the Bass. A group photograph of boys on Lamb Island, now owned by the paranormalist, Uri Geller, is also included.

Pa Evans' photographs of the Isle of May are dated 1911 and do not include any Boy Scouts. It is likely that he made the journey on *P. S. Redgauntlet* in the company of his father, William Evans, the naturalist. The Isle of May is very much nearer to the Fife coast than it is to East Lothian and steamships of the size of *Redgauntlet* would certainly not start out from Canty Bay. It is a long, fairly low-lying island which, in profile, has sometimes been likened to an ocean-going vessel.

Part 4 also includes Canty Bay which in many ways was the spiritual home of Pa Evans. He had been visiting the bay from a very early age but in 1921 he was able to rent one of the small cottages for the sum of £5 per annum, payable in advance. Two years later, in 1923, he purchased the whole of Lower Canty Bay from Sir Hew Hamilton Dalrymple for the sum of £850. Following the death of his mother in 1921 and his father in 1922, he decided to use his inheritance towards

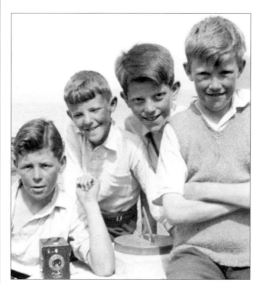

Four boys from the 6th troop gather round the sundial at summer camp, Canty Bay, in 1935. *From left to right:* Jack Cairns (who wrote the Preface for this book); Jimmy Cairns (younger brother of Jack); W. Robertson; and Ian MacLeod.

the purchase price. It was a fitting memorial to the memory of his parents, who, he said, 'took a very kindly interest in the Scouts and Cubs'. In the Evans' archive there are prints, glass negatives and slides covering the many Boy Scout camps that took place at Gullane and Canty Bay. Space permits the inclusion of only a small percentage of the available material. When Pa Evans was a leader in the scout troop attached to the Edinburgh Industrial Brigade Home he took many photographs during their frequent visits to Gullane in the early 1900s. Judging from the inclusion of the Brigade band and a number of rather 'eccentric' characters, they were certainly there to enjoy themselves. Evans' largest collection of Boy Scouts and Cub photographs is of Canty Bay and its environs. For many years the boys from Charlotte Chapel and other organisations enjoyed the unequalled opportunities for experiencing the open air, the natural environment, walking, climbing and sailing, all within a Christian framework. The photograph on page 111 of the Charlotte Chapel scouts with the trek cart in 1921 is particularly interesting as the event was re-enacted by the 66th Leith Scout Group on 26 September 2009. Members pulled the rebuilt original cart a distance of 25 miles from Rose Street in Edinburgh to Canty Bay to raise funds for improvements at Canty Bay.

Part 4 also has early photographs of Canty Bay Hotel and the neighbouring villages of Aberlady and Gullane.

Top left. Evans took this photograph of the Bass Rock and its lighthouse from the *Hermann Sauber* en route for Hamburg in 1906. The lighthouse, designed by the engineer, David Alan Stevenson, and built for just over £8,000, operated from 1 November 1902. Before 1988, when the light was automated, it was lit by means of incandescent gas from high flash point paraffin oil. The light is now monitored remotely from the headquarters of the Northern Lighthouse Board in Edinburgh.

Top right. Evans made a copy of this 1836 notice when he visited the Bass Rock in 1954. Clearly the difficulty of protecting wild life is not a new problem in Scotland. Solan Geese are gannets.

Above left. The compressed air plant for the foghorn on the Bass Rock, photographed in 1910, was installed in 1908.

Right. The foghorn, on the north-east corner of the Bass, was installed in 1908. Its siren was designed to sound three, four-second blasts every two minutes.

The boys of the 6th troop, Charlotte Chapel, land on Craigleith Island in September 1938. The boys are, *from left to right*: Joe Howieson; Bertie Brown; Charlie Brown; Walter Howieson; and Peter Brown. The light-weight craft was built by Pa Evans at Canty Bay. Other photographs of the trip to the island show the boys having lunch and tea before returning to the mainland in the early evening.

Above. There have been three lighthouses on the Isle of May. The first was established in 1635 as a coal-burning iron basket fixed on top of a stone structure. Unfortunately, the intensity and appearance of the flame varied according to the weather. It used 400 tons of coal every year. The second lighthouse (seen in this 1911 photograph) was known as the Low Light, built at the east end of the island in 1844. It was discontinued in 1887 when the North Carr Lightship was installed. For the third lighthouse, see far right.

Right. Evans photographed the Pilgrim's Haven on the Isle of May in 1911. It is said that it was here that many pilgrims arrived 'to pay their vows at the shrine of St Adrian of the May', who died in the year 875. The ruins of the chapel still exist.

Far right. The third, or main, lighthouse that still operates, was designed in a Gothic style by Robert Stevenson in 1816. After the mechanism had been altered on several occasions over the years, it was automated on 31 March 1989.

The steamer *P. S. Redgauntlet* was launched on 4 April 1895 by Barclay, Curle & Co., Glasgow who also built the engine. The vessel was 215 feet long, 22 feet wide and had a gross tonnage of 277. Initially, it was operated on the Clyde by North British Railways but was bought by Galloway Saloon Steam Packet Company, the Forth owners, in May 1909, where it operated until the outbreak of the First World War. Galloway organised cruises to the Isle of May from Portobello, Methil, Ely and North Berwick. The ship was requisitioned by the Admiralty on 23 May 1916 and bought by them on 12 August 1917. After the War, *Redgauntlet* saw service in Algeria, before being deregistered in 1934. Evans' photograph is dated 1911, the year after a landing platform was built on the Isle of May.

The photograph, looking west towards Edinburgh on 22 July 1898,
is of Main Street, Aberlady, near the junction with the Wynd which
leads down to Aberlady Bay. On the left, the two-storey building
with the attic windows was originally the Temperance Hotel.
Because of the acute angle at which the photograph has been
taken, the entrance to the Wynd is barely discernible. It is on the
right between the ivy-covered house with the ornate railings and
the low pantiled cottage with the light-coloured frontage.

Evans photographed this dramatic picture of a wreck at Aberlady Bay on a visit from a scout camp at Gullane in 1903. Fred Hay is balanced precariously at the top of one of the masts and David Addis is on the beach, shouting up to him, presumably warning him to be careful. Evans' additional notes say: 'The wreck was overgrown by seaweed and much worn by the waves which submerged all but the masts at every tide.'

Above. Evans describes this idyllic scene as the Keeper's (gamekeeper's) House, Gosford, on 23 August 1898. In living memory, it has been known as Hungary House but the reason for that has not been discovered. An 1808 map of the area gives the name as 'Hungry House' but in the 1851 Ordnance Survey map the name is 'Hungary'. The buildings are now almost derelict.

Right. The eighteenth-century Aberlady Cross stands on the north pavement of Main Street a few hundred yards west of its junction with the Wynd. The house, hidden behind the foliage on the left, is Cross Cottage, at one time the home of Nigel Tranter, the historical novelist, who died in 2000. The photograph was taken on 22 July 1898.

The village blacksmith, his assistant and perhaps a budding apprentice are photographed at the Old Smiddy, Gullane in August 1903. The building still exists, but is now operated as an attractive gift shop.

Above. Evans describes this photograph as: 'Castle Douglas, residence on Archerfield Links of Dan Douglas and Jessie Cameron, 1912'. The story may well have ended there had it not been for a fairly lengthy entry in volume 3 of Pa Evans' own diaries. The entry runs as follows: 'Dan was a quiet little man, whose principal fault was a total inability to settle down under civilised conditions. A vagrant all his life, he was known, as is usual amongst his class, who are not often legally married, equally by his father's or his mother's surname. Jessie, tempestuous and untamed when sober, she was the terror even of the rough men of her acquaintance when in liquor, a condition liable to occur whenever her slender resources permitted'. Evans also felt obliged to mention that Jessie was from a well-to-do, God-fearing family, her brother being a parish minister near Edinburgh.

Right. Dan Douglas, or Plean, and Jessie Cameron at Gullane Smiddy in 1912.

Left. Camping equipment and provisions arrive at Gullane camp in 1904.

Below left. A good spread has been laid on for visitors' day at Gullane camp in 1903. In the background there are what appear to be fishing nets strung up on poles, possibly for drying before repairs are done.

Below. The Edinburgh Industrial Brigade Home banner, displayed at Gullane in 1910, carries several messages designed to appeal to the higher values of human nature: UNITED WE STAND; WE HOPE TO BE GOOD CITIZENS; WE HELP THOSE WHO TRY TO HELP THEMSELVES; 1909. The banner was painted by James Hargreaves, on the left, and Forrest Myles, on the right.

Above. The members of the band of the Edinburgh Industrial Brigade Home are dressed for the occasion with tuba, horns, euphonium, trombone, cornets and drums at Gullane camp in 1913.

Right. Supplies of food and milk arrive at the Edinburgh Industrial Brigade Home camp at Gullane in 1912.

Above left. Mr R. Black, superintendent, is in the centre of the picture with the assistant superintendent, Mr McMillan, on his left. Unfortunately, the identity of the man in the suit has not been recorded. The photograph was taken at the Edinburgh Industrial Brigade Home camp at Gullane in 1912. The Home was based at No. 72 Grove Street, Edinburgh until 1900, after which it moved to No. 1 Ponton Street.

Above right. The three worthies, at the same camp, are, from left to right: Chinnie Garvin; Pongo McManus; and Mr McMillan.

Left. All 'mod cons' were the order of the day, including this top of the range biscuit box fire-place at Gullane in 1913.

Pongo McManus, the officers' orderly, at the E. I. B. H. camp at
Gullane in 1912.

Chinnie Garvin as the camp policeman at the Gullane
camp in 1912.

Guardsman Garvin, complete with banner, at the same
camp in 1912.

Above. Canty Bay Inn is believed to have been in existence since at least 1870. It is photographed here sometime prior to 1880 when it was owned by the Kendall family. Pa Evans traced the names of the various innkeepers: William B. Kendall, 1870–80; Charles J. Downie, 1880–89; Finlay G. Manson, 1889–92; James Kendall, 1892–98; Colin Mackenzie, 1898–1903; Robert Kirkpatrick, 1903–13; and John Henderson, 1913–17. In 1881, the single-storey building was given an extra storey and other extensions.

In the photograph, the visitor sitting on the bench is pointing the telescope directly at the Bass Rock. Evans copied the original photograph in 1950.

Left. The Canty Bay Hotel wine list for *c.* 1882 is headed by a beautiful view of the bay at a time when the proprietor was Charles J. Downie. It states that the hotel was three miles east of North Berwick and that boat trips were available to the Bass Rock. The wine list included sherry, port. claret, hock, champagne and spirits. The spirits included Scotch Whisky, Irish Whiskey, brandy, Jamaican rum, Hollands and London Old Tom. The cheapest sherry was four shillings (20p) per bottle and the most expensive champagne was eight shillings (40p) per bottle.

Visitors, and their friends, from the nearby
Gullane Point camp arrive at the new
Canty Bay Hotel in 1904. The new hotel
was built, c.1894, at the top of the cliff
adjacent to the road leading to North
Berwick.

Top left. The 6th Charlotte Chapel troop arrive at Canty Bay in July 1938. *From left to right*: Charlie Brown; Joe Howieson; A. Howieson; Bertie Brown; Archie Howieson and Walter Howieson.

Top right. Leaders, including Pa Evans and Jack Cairns to his right, with boys of the 6th cub pack at Canty Bay on 17 July 1952.

Above left. Leaders, with Pa Evans, and the boys of the 119th Granton pack ready to leave Canty Bay after an enjoyable camp, 28 June 1954.

Above right. 6th Baden-Powell Guild of Old Scouts with their families at Canty Bay in 1956.

Boys of the 61st Edinburgh Industrial
Brigade House troop board the *Bonnie
Doon* at Canty Bay in July 1910 ready to
visit the Bass Rock.

In 1921 the boys of the 6th Charlotte Chapel troop take a well-earned rest from pulling the trek cart all the way from Rose Street in Edinburgh to the Canty Bay camp site. Traffic conditions in 1921 were obviously very different from today. In 2009 members of the 66th Leith Scout Group re-enacted the trek by pulling the rebuilt original cart the 25 miles from Rose Street to Canty Bay, to raise funds for improvements at the Bay.

Top left. Kestrels at dinner, with Pa Evans on the left, at Canty Bay in April 1938.
From left to right: W. E. Evans; Bertie Brown; Walter Howieson; Alec Howieson; and K. Fraser.

Top right. 6th Charlotte Chapel troop on the rocks west of Canty Bay in April 1938.

Above left. Tea time on parents' day during the summer camp of the 6th pack, Charlotte Chapel, at Canty Bay, July 1939.

Above right. The young herring gull is being cared for by the boys of the 6th troop, Charlotte Chapel, on a visit to Lamb Island which lies between Fidra and Craigleith, a short distance off shore from North Berwick. The photograph is dated 7 August 1953.

Charlotte Ethel Evans was a
frequent visitor to Canty Bay.
She is seen here in 1951
standing beside her beloved
1926 Morris.

EPILOGUE

William Edgar Evans was a man of many parts and considerable ability. He was born into a fairly well-to-do family, lived in a comfortable house, and had the advantage of being educated at Merchiston Castle School, which, in those days, was at the east end of Colinton Road within walking distance of his home. His father was an actuary and his mother was a highly intelligent member of the famous Deuchar family of Morningside. As a youngster he had several close friends, but as he developed his interests in photography and natural history it is likely that he became more independently-minded than gregarious. For certain, he honed his organisational skills to a high degree and became something of a perfectionist later in life, which set him apart as a natural-born leader. Not only did he not suffer fools gladly, but often he did not suffer them at all.

Evans died in 1963 at the age of 79, but his legacy has lived on in the particular spheres of interest in which he lived his life. He qualified as a Bachelor of Science at Edinburgh University with distinction in botany, and, after service with the Royal Army Medical Corps during the First World War (where he reached the rank of captain) he devoted his working life to the study of plants at the Royal Botanic Garden Edinburgh. In the world of botany, the name Evans (including his father and grandfather) ranks among the country's leading botanists. Evans was made a fellow of the Royal Society Edinburgh for his services to botany. During the First World War he saw service in Mesopotamia (now Iraq) and Persia (now Iran). At the time, he was keen to serve his country in whatever way he was best suited, but after the War, and long before the outbreak of the Second World War, he became a pacifist.

From an early age, Evans developed an interest in photography, encouraged by both his father and his mother. Indeed it seems to have become something of a family hobby as father, mother and sister, Ethel, all joined in on photographic outings, especially to areas of Edinburgh, south of the family home in Morningside Park. In addition to the photographs that Evans took, both sides of the family amassed a large number of family portraits. Best of all was their discipline in dating and annotating the photographs with names and locations. Only occasionally did they lapse into the local historian's nightmare of describing a superb photograph as 'Auntie Maggie' without dating it or identifying *whose* Auntie Maggie. The wealth of material on both the Evans and the Deuchar sides of the family was such, however, that by a process of elimination and comparison, it was possible to identify almost all of the photographs. No such shortcomings were found in Evans' own photographic records. Almost every glass slide and glass negative was dated, annotated and indexed, but, of course, many years later, and without being party to his personal knowledge of the events, it can be difficult to appreciate the relationships between some of the people and the events. The Evans photographic archive is undoubtedly a major contribution to the Edinburgh scene and deserves to be better known.

Evans was 26 years of age in 1908 when Lord Baden-Powell began the Boy Scout Movement in England. He was, therefore, never a cub or a scout but in later life he became very involved, particularly with the 6th troop attached to Charlotte Chapel. He accepted the position of scoutmaster in 1920 but unfortunately decided to resign two years later following the death of his parents. He did, however, feel able to accept the position of honorary scoutmaster which gave him the chance to assist without the day-to-day strain of being in charge. It is not known why Evans attended Charlotte Chapel rather than the original Morningside Parish Church where his mother, father and sister worshipped. Perhaps he wanted to be independent of them or perhaps he found more inspiration from one minister than the other.

After his purchase of Canty Bay in 1923, Evans spent most of the summer months living there, travelling each day on his Coventry Eagle motor cycle to his work at the Royal Botanic Garden at Inverleith. In 1936 he established the Evans Trust for Boys and transferred the Canty Bay property and a maintenance endowment to the trustees to be used 'for Christian Recreational Training'. During the Second World War, Canty Bay (excluding the east cottages which were tenanted) was out of bounds even to the trustees as it was requisitioned by the War Department as Royal Navy Station No. 3. At the end of the War, the trustees were awarded the princely sum of £47 to compensate them for the extensive damage done to the property. In 1956 Pa Evans suffered a heart attack that was sufficiently serious to require his sister, Ethel, to continue to reside with him at Canty Bay in the summer months. Early in 1963 he became more seriously ill and died on 21 March 1963 in Strathearn Nursing Home in Edinburgh.

After the death of Pa Evans, Ethel took over the job of chairing the Trust meetings until her own death in 1970. Jack Cairns, group scoutmaster at Charlotte Chapel from 1958 until 1975, became a trustee on the death of Pa Evans in 1963: he became chairman on the death of Ethel in 1970 and resigned in 1991. Little did Jack know that 40 years later he would be asked to write the Preface for this short photographic record of the life of 'Pa'.

Canty Bay in May 1934.

INDEX